Restoring the Warrior

A guide for Veteran and First Responder wellness

Second Edition
Revised

By

Dr. Benjamin Iobst, US Army Combat Veteran, Retired Law Enforcement Officer

Restoring the Warrior 2nd ed.

With Contributions by

Justin Wright, USMC Combat Veteran
Jeremy Gann, US Army Combat Veteran
Matthew Rush, Retired Law Enforcement Officer
Christopher Schierloh, Paramedic
Adam Perreault, US Navy Veteran, Firefighter

Weekly Reflections by

Bethany Adams, Law Enforcement Officer
Jennifer Aleman, US Army Combat Veteran (War on Terror)
David Alercia, USMC Veteran, Retired Law Enforcement Officer
William Carver, Paramedic, Former Firefighter
Thomas J. Carson, US Air Force Veteran
Chuck Durback, US Army Combat Veteran (Vietnam War)
Jeremy Gann, US Army Veteran (Iraq and Afghanistan War)
Christopher Hendricks, Law Enforcement Officer, Paramedic
John Hill, USMC Combat Veteran (Desert Storm), Retired Law Enforcement Officer
Amy J. Iobst, EMT
Jason Kesack, Law Enforcement Officer
John Kukitz, US Army Combat Veteran (Vietnam War)
James LaFey, US Air Force Veteran (Iraq and Afghanistan Wars)
Nate Laskey, USMC Combat Veteran (Iraq War)
Kevin McCloud, US Army Veteran
Kate Murray, Law Enforcement Officer
Adam Perreault, US Navy Veteran, Professional Firefighter
Freddie Reed, US Army Combat Veteran (Iraq War)
Dr. Thomas Ritter, US Army Veteran, Retired Law Enforcement Officer
Matthew Rush, Retired Law Enforcement Officer
Brian Sabo, Former Law Enforcement Officer
Shane Schmeckenbecher, US Army Combat Veteran (Iraq War), Probation Officer
Christopher Schierloh, Paramedic
Kenny Seagraves, US Navy Veteran
Robert Smith, US Army Combat Veteran (Desert Storm and Iraq War)
Trevor Tasetano, USMC Combat Veteran (Iraq War), Former Volunteer Firefighter
Drew Taylor, Probation Officer
John Turoczi, Retired Law Enforcement Officer
Justin Wright, USMC Combat Veteran (Iraq War)

Restoring the Warrior 2nd ed.

Restoring the Warrior: A Guide to Veteran and First Responder Wellness – Second Edition

Softcover ISBN: 979-8-9948051-0-7

Hardcover ISBN:979-8-9948051-1-4

KDP Softcover ISBN: 9798264434488

KDP Hardcover ISBN: 9798264434815

First Edition Published 2025

Revised: April 2026

Written By: Benjamin Iobst, Ph.D.

Contributions By: Justin Wright; Jeremy Gann; Matthew Rush; Christopher Schierloh; Adam Perreault; Bethany Adams; Jennifer Aleman; David Alercia; William Carver; Thomas J. Carson; Chuck Durback; Christopher Hendricks; John Hill; Amy J. Iobst; Jason Kesack; John Kukitz; James LaFey; Nate Laskey; Kevin McCloud; Kate Murray; Freddie Reed; Dr. Thomas Ritter; Brian Sabo; Shane Schmeckenbecher; Kenny Seagraves; Robert Smith; Trevor Tasetano; Drew Taylor; John Turoczi

Independently Published: BTI Consulting Services

For permission, contact:

BTI Consulting Services

Email: Biobst@bticonsultingservice.com

This book is a work of nonfiction. Names, organizations, and events are portrayed accurately to the best of the author's knowledge. Any therapeutic or wellness guidance is offered from the perspective of lived and professional experience but does not substitute for clinical medical or mental health advice.

Restoring the Warrior 2nd ed.

Table of Contents

About the Second Edition

The first edition of this book, as well as the fantastic work being done by purpose-driven First Responders and Veterans, has had an amazing effect. In our region, we have seen dozens of Veterans and First Responders coming together at meetings to begin to grow, heal, and find purpose. From these gatherings, we have had many inquiries about how to create local meetings centered around posttraumatic growth, and recommendations for best practices on how those meetings should be conducted.

This second edition contains all of the information needed to create those spaces for growth. This edition contains several chapters at the end of this book that detail the mission, execution, and framework of posttraumatic growth meetings, or as we're calling them locally, Tribe of the Restored Warrior, Posttraumatic Growth Meetings. We've also included a section of reflections from some of the original attendees at these growth meetings to help provide topics for the meeting and to share the journey of growth with a broader warrior audience.

Keep up the good fight and continue forward with purpose and growth!

Acknowledgments

This book would not have been possible without the unwavering support, guidance, and inspiration from so many incredible individuals and organizations. First and foremost, I want to express my deepest gratitude to my family, friends, and former leaders whose encouragement, patience, and understanding have been my foundation throughout this journey. Your belief in me has been a constant source of strength.

A heartfelt thank you to Eastern PA EMS CISM and the Tri-County CISM Team for their dedication to providing critical incident stress management and peer support to First Responders. Your work is invaluable in ensuring that those who serve our communities have the resources and support they need to heal and thrive.

To Vets and Badges, your mission of bridging the gap between Veterans and First Responders is an inspiration. Your commitment to fostering resilience and wellness among those who have served is making a profound impact, and I am honored to acknowledge your efforts.

I also extend my appreciation to Boulder Crest Foundation, whose innovative and transformative approach to mental health and training has been life-changing for many in our community, through the Struggle Well and Warrior Pathh programs. Your dedication to posttraumatic growth and holistic healing is a beacon of hope for warriors seeking restoration.

To the many organizations of Veterans and First Responders who have helped our community heal, your work has not gone unnoticed. Keep up the good work. Additionally, to the many professionals who have made it their mission to serve the First Responder and Veteran communities, a heartfelt thank you.

A special thank you to the LVLEO Team and LVLEO Providers, who continue to champion the well-being of law enforcement officers by providing essential resources and support. Your efforts to ensure that First Responders receive the mental health care they need are truly commendable.

Finally, to all First Responders and military Veterans, this book is for you. Your courage, sacrifice, and commitment to service do not go unnoticed. You are the backbone of our communities, and your well-being matters. I hope the insights shared in this book help you find balance, healing, and strength in your journey forward.

Lastly, this book is formatted and written for maximum accessibility in the First Responder and Veteran community. The larger font size is designed to be easy to read by our older Veterans and First Responders, as well as the members of our warrior community with brain injuries or severe PTSD. The spacing between lines allows for easy note-taking and highlighting as needed.

Thank you all for your support, your dedication, and your service.

Introduction

Members of the military, Veterans, and First Responders are a unique breed. We are the ones who run toward danger-whether it be war, robberies, fires, or car crashes. This calling is often strong at first, but when faced with the harsh realities of what people do to each other and the frustrating politics of "protecting the flock," disillusionment sets in, and burnout begins.

While burnout is common in many professions, those staffed by warriors face it faster and more intensely because we are exposed to the hottest flames. Many times, I've wondered whether the experiences we endure leave us fundamentally different from the society we swore to protect. I believe the answer is yes. We are changed, but we are not broken.

We live in a culture that watches movies about war, crime, and tragedy for entertainment. Yet, when the public encounters these realities in life, or the professionals who live and work in them, many people turn away or declare the trauma “too much” to bear. Many grow to fear those who protect them.

Despite how intimidating we may appear to others, we are deeply giving people. We ignore our own problems to help strangers, our communities, and our country. But the problems we ignore-whether psychological trauma, physical injuries, or a destruction of our very sense of duty-take their toll.

When society views us as “broken,” it too often ignores us, relegating Veterans to VA hospitals or abruptly tossing First Responders out of their roles when they can no longer serve. This contributes to shockingly high suicide rates, a life expectancy for First Responders that is 21 years shorter than the national average, and a life expectancy for Veterans that is 9 years shorter.

This raises an important question: how does a warrior stay healthy and sane in a society that glorifies actors who portray us but often ignores the plight of the real us? The answer is both complicated and simple. We must seek out the best treatments, science, and programs that modern society has created. But we must also educate our society about who we really are: their protectors, but also human.

How do we do this? We do it as we were designed and trained to do, together. Contrary to media portrayals of lone war heroes and First Responders, those of us who have served know one simple truth: we accomplish our hardest tasks as a team. When we bring order to chaos on the streets, we do it as a team. When we deploy to war, we do it as a team.

In nearly all of our most difficult missions, we rely on the person next to us to help achieve the seemingly impossible. But when we suffer, when we hurt, and when we try to heal, we often do it alone. This is where the solution begins to emerge: we cannot recover alone.

We are pack animals. By helping each other carry the weight, we can help each other heal. However, it's important to note that I'm not suggesting we isolate as teams or form militias in the mountains. What I'm proposing-and what this book outlines- is how we can act as peer supports for one another. We can seek out the best doctors, therapists, specialists, and programs for our unique needs, and then share them, supporting one another in our restoration.

Athletes and many other groups have specialized medical programs tailored to their lives and ways of thinking. Why, then, isn't this common for Veterans and First Responders? The reason is that we haven't approached it as united peer groups-not only seeking out experts but also becoming those experts for one another.

This book is a collection of advice and experience aimed at building a tribe of restored warriors-one that begins to change those statistics. In the following chapters, we will discuss how to focus on your individual mental and physical wellness, how to help other Veterans and First Responders become healthier, how to build a peer support network, and how to identify trustworthy medical and specialty providers who truly understand our unique population.

Finally, I believe it is essential to share the perspectives of other Veterans and First Responders in order to begin the discussion of communally healing our culture. Therefore, please take the time to read through the next several sections, which include the thoughts of several warriors who have made wellness a priority in their lives and our culture.

Matt's Perspective

A lot can be said about those who serve on the front lines-both overseas and at home. Regarding police officers, President Calvin Coolidge once said, "*No one is compelled to choose the profession of a police officer, but having chosen it, everyone is obliged to live up to the standard of its requirements.*" That standard has always been, at its core, to serve and protect the citizenry with honor and integrity. It requires maintaining a balance between the negatives and positives of the very society they serve.

Public opinion varies, but contrary to what the media might have us believe, the vast majority of men and women who serve their communities do, in fact, embody that standard.

Think about it: someone who willingly chooses a career knowing full well they will witness some of the worst humanity has to offer, and may be required to lay down their life for a coworker or a stranger, doesn’t, at first glance, sound like someone of sound mind. Yet this is what countless men and women do every day. They suit up, step onto the front lines, and willingly place themselves in harm's way for their communities and their country. They do it even though most could never fully comprehend what they were signing up for.

There is, however, a growing epidemic within the First Responder and military communities, especially when it comes to how they care for themselves, particularly their mental health. The rates of substance abuse, divorce, premature death, and suicide do not lie, and if anything, they are underreported. We ask so much of those who serve, yet many fail to realize the immense physical and emotional toll these roles can take. Few understand all that First Responders are asked to witness, absorb, and carry with them.

The real tragedy is that many of the people who don't fully understand the toll... are the ones doing the job. They spend so much time focusing outward on the evil and chaos in the world that they often fail to recognize the darkness quietly building within themselves. It's not easy for someone trained to maintain control in any situation to admit they may no longer be able to help themselves. But sadly, that is often the reality they face.

The very traits that make them exceptional on the streets-stoicism, decisiveness, resilience-can be the same ones that make it hard to acknowledge or confront personal struggles. Combine that with a culture that has historically minimized reactions to stress, stigmatized mental health issues like depression and anxiety, and even removed those suffering from active duty roles, and it's no wonder the profession is in crisis. Add in the old "suck it up" and "stuff it down" mentality, and you get a recipe for internal collapse.

But there is hope.

The first step toward solving any issue is recognizing that one exists. Thankfully, we are witnessing a cultural shift-a more open and compassionate approach to mental health, substance abuse, and other challenges. The stigmas are slowly being dismantled, and proactive strategies (many of which are covered in this book) are being embraced. But it all starts with recognition.

The most powerful tool available to us is one that has long served officers well in other contexts: calling for backup. Having a support network made up of those who've done the job, lived the life, and faced similar challenges can be invaluable. When that desire to help others is backed by additional training-often accompanied by confidentiality protections-it creates a powerful internal resource within departments.

Now, more than ever, we must take care of our own. We must show up for one another. First Responders need to know they are not alone-not in what they've experienced, not in what they're going through now, and not in what they may face in the future. Even more importantly, they need to know they are not alone in healing. That they have trusted companions walking with them on the journey to a better present-and a better future.

This is what must become part of the new "standard" for police officers.

-Matthew Rush, Retired Law Enforcement Officer

How It Started

To fully understand the advice and insights in this book, it's essential to know the backstory-one that includes my own journey.

I joined the U.S. Army straight out of high school, enlisting as an infantryman, motivated by the events of 9/11. Shortly after completing initial entry training, I was deployed to Iraq for combat operations. At first, I found this confusing-I had joined expecting to fight Al Qaeda in Afghanistan. Several combat tours and countless crazy-and sometimes horrible-experiences later, I found myself leaving the military with an honorable discharge, determined to make a difference back home.

At the urging of my parents, who wanted me to channel my military training into something positive, and driven by my own desire to help others, I was drawn back into a life of service-this time, in law enforcement.

I became a police officer in a city of about 125,000 people with a moderately high violent crime rate. Over time, I served in various roles, including patrol, investigations, hostage negotiation, and supervisory positions.

During my early years in policing, I ignored my mental and physical wellness. Gradually, the accumulation of past traumas and present stressors took a toll. It started subtly: high blood pressure, a little weight gain, and a beer at night to help me sleep better. Before I knew it, I was both a physical and psychological wreck, and I didn't even realize it-I had never taken the time to look inward.

Fortunately, I was blessed with an amazing family with generations of military service, role models in law enforcement who recognized the harm we were doing to ourselves, and supportive friends who understood the need for healthy recovery. With their support, I was able to regain my mental and physical health.

Along the way, I connected with other First Responders and Veterans who were also striving for balance and health in their lives. Together, we started small: first a support group, then a wellness team, and eventually training programs. By building partnerships with healthcare providers, regional agencies, First Responder leadership, volunteers, and advocacy groups, we created a regional peer wellness team that now serves 1,500 First Responders and directly supports over 100 individuals in need each year.

Early in this journey, we learned one critical lesson: we cannot do this alone. This book is designed to walk you through the mindset and processes necessary to build health and resilience, not only as individuals but also as agencies and as a culture of First Responders and Veterans.

Individual Wellness

Self-care is an essential part of living a long and healthy life. But how do we implement self-care when our professions have taught us that our personal safety comes second to the welfare of others? This question lies at the root of many issues surrounding mental wellness, physical wellness, and achieving balance in our personal lives. Our nature tells us to put others first, our training reinforces this mindset, and as a result, we often put our own needs last.

To create meaningful change, we must recognize that we cannot effectively perform our jobs or live fulfilling lives without prioritizing our wellness equally to the care we provide for others. From a group perspective, ensuring the well-being of our peers-whether they are Veterans or First Responders- can help foster this shift. By looking out for the welfare of our brothers and sisters in arms, we create a culture of mutual care. As mentioned in the preceding chapter, we are social beings designed to function as a team. Just as we care for each other when wounded on the battlefield, we must maintain that same mentality when it comes to mental and physical health. This approach can help improve life expectancy and quality of life across the board.

It is essential that we maintain a healthy outlook and a healthy culture, both as Veterans and First Responders and as individuals. One critical way to achieve this is by keeping our minds organized as we navigate our work and daily lives. A key practice in maintaining mental clarity is making it a priority in our lives. Ensuring that we add a mental wellness practice such as box breathing, meditation, practicing gratitude or many other techniques can have profound effects on our lives and those around us.

Also, our mind can become cluttered with past grudges, negative experiences, and unhealthy patterns, similarly to old physical injuries. If we do not actively clean out our mental file cabinets through therapy, wellness practices, and positive habits, we build up emotional and mental clutter. When a crisis-our proverbial mental injury-hits, this mental hoarding can make it much harder to cope and heal. By regularly clearing out old burdens, we can prevent ourselves from becoming overwhelmed and emotionally unstable when challenges arise.

Adam's Perspective

The life of a firefighter and their families operates around "ON (work) and OFF (family or personal time)" shifts. Every day, month, and year is designed and managed based on being ON or OFF shift. When you factor in overtime or events, it becomes very confusing for everyone involved, often leading to personal and professional conflicts. When I talk about conflicts in managing our ON and OFF shift schedules, they become complicated by stress and trauma.

Firefighters' stress arises from trying to balance a chaotic and confusing ON and OFF schedule. The origin of family stress shares the same conflict, but it becomes compounded by their daily life experiences. As firefighters, we are trained to take on others' stress in the form of mitigating emergencies. We tend to look at and deal with our home life in the same manner, as we do this to help bring our families or personal lives peace. That's our job as loving spouses, parents, or in self-care. In absorbing this stress, we carry it with us when we go back ON shift.

When we go back ON shift, we conduct a shift change turnover with the OFF-going shift. Typically, these conversations take place at a large, family-style table over coffee. During the shift change, we discuss emergency responses, operational changes, and equipment updates that the OFF-going shift experienced. Emergency responses can range from assisting with pet troubles to handling mass casualty incidents-so too are the experienced traumas. This is where OFF-shift stresses and ON-shift experiences become confusing yet clear when we address firefighter mental health.

The large coffee table is where our mental health challenges often form, but it is also where we can start to address them. When we share our ON-shift experiences, we also share our collective challenges. This sharing also applies to our OFF-shift stresses. As we turn over our ON and OFF shift experiences, we naturally try to help solve each other's issues. Sometimes the solutions aren't constructive, but there's always someone there to redirect us toward a more positive path.

The ON and OFF shift turnover is a fundamental, first step in peer support. As brothers and sisters who have spent most of our adult lives together, we have a unique perspective and understanding of each other. We have been through calls together that didn't go as planned. We recognize each other's struggles to process ON-shift and OFF-shift experiences-or when the stress and trauma from both converge. Taking those first steps at the table, progressing through Peer Support, helps us give our brothers and sisters a way to immediately decompress and better manage the emotional rollercoaster of ON and OFF duty life.

-Adam Perreault, US Navy Veteran, Firefighter

Physical Wellness

The first step toward achieving balance is ensuring we are physically well. Many of us equate physical wellness with simply going to the gym, but it goes far beyond that. The stress we endure can have lasting effects on our bodies, including contributing to cardiac issues and other health problems. Therefore, getting yearly physicals and following medical advice are critical steps. If you are nursing an injury, seeking physical therapy or medical intervention is essential to prevent long-term damage.

Of course, staying in physical shape and exercising is important. However, it cannot end there. We maintain our physical prowess not just for ourselves but to serve others. Unfortunately, we often assume that physical fitness is the only thing that matters. I have seen officers who appear physically fit but suffer from various other health issues. In some cases, I have even witnessed officers come to work while actively experiencing a heart attack.

Too often, we ignore injuries and carry on, promising ourselves that we will address them "later." Some of us overlook high blood pressure, high cholesterol, or other ailments to avoid missing work. Over time, these seemingly small oversights compound and ultimately lower our life expectancy. We convince ourselves that we will deal with them later, during time off, after retirement, or post-deployment, but that "later" rarely comes. This mindset creates a culture of the "walking wounded," with individuals pushing through while their health silently deteriorates.

On the Veteran side, many Veterans are told that they are broken. They have injuries that limit their ability to exercise and enjoy a good quality of life. As a result, they often believe they cannot improve and resign themselves to receiving treatment at the VA, accepting that they can no longer physically do the things they once could. While limitations are real in many capacities, there is always more we can do. Getting involved with a healthy group of individuals can help Veterans become healthier and more active within their limitations and capabilities.

This cycle must stop within the Veteran and First Responder communities. The toll on our health is killing us at an alarming rate, and it is time to make a change. Seeking culturally competent physicians, physical therapists, and other specialists who understand the unique challenges faced by military personnel, Veterans, and First Responders is crucial. By working with professionals who truly grasp our experiences, we can begin to build healthier habits and create a culture of wellness.

Sharing information about these resources is equally important. If you find a culturally competent doctor or specialist who supports the mission of wellness, let others in your social circle of Veterans and First Responders know. By spreading the word, we can ensure that more people in our community receive the care and support they need to thrive.

Mental Wellness

Mental wellness goes far beyond simply coping with what we have experienced and trying to find balance in our lives. It involves putting principles into practice to become healthier and grow from our experiences. This may sound daunting-how can we take trauma and horrible experiences and turn them into something positive? The key is to change our perspective on trauma and stress in small, manageable steps.

The first thing we must embrace is the fact that we are definitely not broken. We are changed by our experiences and may have a different outlook than the rest of society, but we are not broken. By truly understanding and embracing this, we can begin to heal and grow. We do not do this alone. We find others like us, First Responders and Veterans, who also want to live healthier, happier lives.

Next, we must begin to shift our perspective on our experiences. Trauma is real and can have lasting consequences, but the way we look at it can drastically affect its impact on us. I often hear the analogy of a boulder that, when viewed from a distance, reveals itself to be only a pebble. This is an excellent example of how changing our perspective can help us see our experiences from a healthier viewpoint.

Another critical step is learning to repurpose our difficulties into something positive. Life provides us with fuel-both in the form of positive experiences and negative experiences. We can choose to handle that fuel in one of two ways. We can harness it, repurposing it to power our personal growth, motivation, and positive contributions, or we can scatter it carelessly, creating fire hazards in different areas of our lives-allowing our pain, anger, or frustration to spread unchecked. The choice is entirely ours. How we process, use, and direct our life's experiences determines whether they will empower us or consume us.

It is also important to discuss grit versus mental wellness. Many of us in the Veteran and First Responder communities have an abundance of grit-the ability to endure and push through extremely difficult events. While grit is essential, it is not the same as mental wellness. Grit helps us withstand pain, whereas mental wellness and resilience provide us with the wisdom to know when to take a break and heal.

This parallels the conversation about physical wellness. Real healing begins when we learn to take care of ourselves and show ourselves rest, patience, and compassion. Grit is crucial in emergencies, but our professions and lives can be greatly enhanced by focusing on mental wellness and resilience.

A key element of mental wellness is having a strong support structure. While practices like rest and perspective-shifting are valuable, there will be times when life becomes overwhelming. This is when a support system becomes essential. Building and maintaining healthy relationships with supportive individuals is key to resilience.

Humans are social creatures who thrive when working together. Allowing someone to help carry the weight during tough times can be incredibly helpful, and we can return the favor when they are in need. This mutual support is where real change begins within our First Responder and Veteran communities.

We must also end the era of the "silent struggle," where First Responders and Veterans are only seen as valuable when their bodies and minds are strong. We are human beings who will experience physical and mental injuries. Embracing this reality and showing compassion for one another is essential. While many of us wish society treated us better, we often fail to show that same care to each other. How can we expect society to care for us if we don't care for one another?

Jeremy's Perspective

I experienced combat three times during the early years of our nation's "war on terrorism". The first two were 82nd Airborne deployments to Afghanistan in 2003 and Iraq in 2004. Both could be labelled as "normal," so far as infantry deployments to a combat zone go. Short periods of fighting mixed in with longer periods of guard duty, card playing, and boredom. I then deployed back to Iraq in 2006 as part of Task Force Bandit, a spearhead element in the "second battle of Ramadi". The fighting was more fierce, relentless, and lasted for a longer duration than anything I had experienced on previous deployments. It was also in a highly populated urban area, a true 360-degree battlefield. Like numerous others, some of the events I experienced left lasting impressions (or traumas) on my mind, body, and spirit. This realization has taken many years to identify and begin healing. The great news for all of us is that there are many paths to healing. The Tao Te Ching appropriately suggests that "a journey of a thousand miles begins with a single step."

I spent much of the next decade plus "suffering silently," which basically means enduring emotional pain without expressing it openly or seeking treatment. My case involved quickly reintegrating into life at home as a father of two young girls after spending over a year in a particularly dangerous part of Iraq. Initially, I lacked the awareness to realize what a serious problem I had brewing within. I was experiencing varying degrees of emotional dysregulation happening within me and a mixed bag of results in my life. Hyper-vigilance, anxiety, anger, alcohol abuse, and depression were constants. I began with talk therapy, which was a tremendous tool but not an end. I also took a variety of medications that were prescribed to treat the symptoms I was experiencing. I had medications for depression, anxiety, sleep, and lack of focus, just to name a few. Many of us must reach "rock bottom" before we realize how unsustainable our current model is. Far too many chose to end their journey here and take their life. I considered it myself on more than one occasion. Thankfully, instead, I was introduced to some new tools, such as meditation and mindful breathing, that helped to re-frame my perspective and bring a sense of peace to my inner environment.

Whatever the chosen path toward peace and wellness, it must include an honest look inward. We need to take individual accountability for behaviors that do not serve us and often create chaos and suffering in our lives. One of the pioneers of psychotherapy, Carl Jung, suggested that "until you make the unconscious conscious, it will direct your life, and you will call it fate". It is through this inward journey where posttraumatic growth, transformation and enlightenment occur.

One of the primary drivers of my personal transformation has been incorporating meditation and mindful breathing exercises into my life.

Neuroplasticity refers to our brain's ability to create new neural networks and pathways. Meditation can help us foster an inner environment that is conducive to creating these new pathways. It is possible to still our minds in a way that can truly shift our perspective of ourselves and the world around us. There is also tremendous connectivity between the mind and our breath. The simple act of slow, mindful breathing takes what is normally an autonomic function and makes it conscious for a short period of time. These types of practice create the inner space needed to become responsive and deliberate rather than reactive to external stimuli.

There is a Hindu proverb that states, "There are many paths up the mountain, all leading to the top. The only ones wasting time are those who run in circles around the mountain, telling others that their path is wrong." This is true of spiritual practice, and it is true regarding our path to healing. There are many programs, tools, and techniques available. Find what works for you and lean in.

-Jeremy Gann, US Army Combat Veteran

Helping Others and Working Together

We have already touched on the importance of taking care of one another several times, but I want to emphasize it again. First Responders and Veterans are individuals trained and experienced in functioning as a cohesive and efficient team. This means that the most dangerous and complex tasks we undertake are always done together.

This principle also applies when one of us is struggling. Time and time again, I have seen the First Responder and Veteran communities rally around individuals in need. And who better to help than those who truly understand? But how do we foster a culture where reaching out for help with internal and personal challenges becomes the norm?

The first step is understanding why we hesitate to seek help. By nature, we are helpers, not those who ask for help. We rush into dangerous situations without hesitation because that's our role. However, when we find ourselves in need, it often feels like a sign of weakness or an undue burden on those around us. This is completely untrue. True strength lies in knowing when to ask for help, but this requires education and a shift in mindset.

Many of us are trained to ignore red flags and push forward. While this makes us excellent at our jobs, it also makes it difficult to recognize when we are not doing well. We are conditioned to run toward danger while others recoil from it, making it inherently challenging to assess our own well-being. Additionally, pride and training often come into play. For example, if our house were on fire, many of us would first grab a fire extinguisher or a garden hose rather than immediately calling 911. Yet, if we saw our buddy's house on fire, we would call for backup without hesitation. This demonstrates why it's so important to check in on one another: we are more likely to notice and act on others' struggles than our own.

What I am advocating for is the development of a Veteran and First Responder culture that prioritizes checking in on each other. By actively taking steps to ensure everyone is okay, we can reinforce the bond of mutual care. Most of us would give the shirts off our backs to help a buddy; the key is to promote this behavior and cultivate the wisdom to accept help when it's offered.

With this in mind, we must recognize that we can share strengths, resilience, and resources with each other as a culture of warriors. Locally, we have combined our wellness team approach to include all segments of the warrior community, which includes Law Enforcement, EMS, Fire, Veterans, and First Responders such as Coroners and Corrections. Through this approach we see the sharing of strengths and healthy perspectives across branches, the growth of a warrior wellness culture that is not "owned" or territorial. This sharing and collaboration is key, as together we become a powerhouse of change.

To achieve this, two things must happen. First, we need to understand that needing help is not a sign of failure. Most of us eagerly help others but instinctively decline help when offered. Developing the understanding that it's okay not to "have it all together" is crucial. Recognizing that we are stronger as a team, rather than struggling alone, is key.

So, how do we accomplish this within a culture that constantly pushes us to our limits? The first step is promoting care for one another and practicing positivity as much as we focus on identifying threats. In our training, we are taught to identify dangers and always stay alert, which naturally leads us to focus on negatives. It is essential that we also make a conscious effort to identify and practice positivity in our interactions and lives. What we practice is what we become good at-so if we only practice negativity, we will excel at it.

One practice I use in my personal life combines positivity, self-care, and communication. My buddies and I have a group chat where we share one thing we are grateful for each day and one thing we plan to do for self-care. This practice fosters positive thinking, encourages self-care, and keeps us connected. At first, it may feel awkward, but over time, it becomes natural, and you'll start noticing more positive things in life.

This daily practice has another benefit: it helps us identify when someone might need support. If a buddy stops participating in the chat or begins sharing concerning messages like, "I'm just glad I woke up today," or "My self-care is not losing it on anyone," it's a sign that we need to rally around them. This is not the only way to build positivity, but it's an effective starting point.

Finally, I want to discuss compassionate accountability. We often protect each other in unhealthy ways. For instance, if a buddy is drinking heavily and missing work, we may think it's our job to cover for them. Unfortunately, this approach can cause more harm than good. Compassionate accountability means holding each other to a standard of care, much like we would with a sibling or close family member. It's about wanting the best for one another and stepping in when necessary.

If a friend is engaging in harmful behaviors, we don't remain silent or push them away. Instead, we address the issue, offer help, and stand by their side as they work to improve. This balance of care and accountability is essential for fostering a healthy and supportive culture.

By practicing positivity daily, we can change the way we think as individuals and, in turn, influence our broader culture. This shift is reinforced by consistently checking in on each other and addressing issues with compassionate accountability instead of criticism. Together, we can create an environment where seeking and offering help are seen as acts of strength, not weakness.

How Do We Change a Culture That Requires Self-Sacrifice?

The nature of the military and First Responder professions inherently requires a high level of selfless service. It's this very mindset that enables professionals to excel at their work-to run toward gunfire, enter burning buildings, and face life-threatening situations head-on. But is it possible to maintain this culture of selflessness while also ensuring proper care for First Responders, military personnel, and Veterans?

I truly believe the answer is yes. We can create a healthier culture within the First Responder and Veteran community while preserving their unmatched ability to perform their mission. This can be achieved through a top-down and bottom-up approach.

From the top down, leaders must actively promote self-care, provide training on personal wellness, and ensure that they themselves model healthy behaviors. A culture shift starts with leaders who prioritize both mission success and the well-being of their personnel.

From the bottom up, resilience and wellness awareness must be integrated into initial entry training. Instilling these values from the beginning ensures that the next generation of First Responders and military personnel grows with a balanced understanding of selflessness and self-care.

By addressing both ends of the spectrum, the culture can begin to shift. Ideally, this approach could also extend life expectancy for those in these professions, moving the needle beyond the alarming average of 57 years.

It is also essential to move beyond the idea that each individual group or agency must address wellness alone. By collaborating regionally, local Police, Fire, EMS, and Veteran groups can form a united wellness team, making sustainable strides toward a healthier culture. This unified approach ensures that progress toward wellness continues, regardless of funding, political motivations, or staffing. Additionally, it allows groups to share motivation, resources, and champions, ensuring that no area, group, or agency is left behind.

Justin's Perspective

The Tribe or Unit-whatever term resonates with you-is the most important factor in continuing a life of wellness and recovery. I've made some of the worst decisions of my life on my own. Now, try making a bad decision after sharing it with others. I believe the chances of making that mistake decrease significantly once we verbalize our thoughts to those we trust.

The second part of the tribe is reconnecting-the connection we once experienced in the military or a platoon of officers. This is what I needed again: the ability to tell jokes, laugh at ourselves, and trust that, no matter what happens, someone will be there to help. A warrior alone is a wasteful thing; a warrior connected is a force for good.

When we defeat negative self-talk, moral injury, or personal struggles by sharing them with our tribe, they become the tribe's struggle. We are no longer alone in the fight.

The hardships ahead-or those behind us-hold value. Turning our struggles into experiences that can be used to help others is a shift in perspective that allows us to embrace the road ahead. Nothing alone is the answer to finding our way back home.

-Justin K. Wright, USMC Combat Veteran, Iraq War

The Importance of Healthy Leadership

To lead effectively, leaders must first self-reflect. Many have been taught unhealthy leadership styles, which are then passed down to the next generation simply because "that's the way it's always been done." At face value, these methods may seem effective-the mission gets accomplished, and success is achieved. However, the deeper question remains: Are we truly taking care of our people if their life expectancy is 21 years shorter than the general population?

Each of us can draw our own conclusions, but the numbers speak volumes. If leaders genuinely care for their troops, addressing this disparity must become a priority.

The solutions to creating a healthier profession are not mysteries-they already exist. Sports medicine has long studied how to keep athletes healthy and high-performing, while industrial-organizational psychology has spent over a century refining methods to improve morale and workplace health. In recent years, the military has started leveraging insights from both fields to enhance the well-being of its members. This progress is commendable and should continue. It is time for the First Responder community to follow suit.

Consider the example of shift staffing. In the 1910s, industrial-organizational psychologists found that fast swing shifts-where workers frequently change hours or shifts within a short period-were detrimental to both health and morale. By implementing steady shifts or longer swing shifts (e.g., one month per shift type before switching), organizations saw a significant increase in workplace safety and employee satisfaction.

So why, over 110 years later, are fast swing shifts still prevalent in the First Responder community despite clear evidence of their harm?

Another question to ask and consider is the use of sick time. Many First Responder agencies have issues where time off for sickness is causing personnel issues. This is generally curbed through bonuses for low sick time usage, or discipline when sick time is overused. As a culture we should consider "wellness days" as wellness is the opposite of sickness. Designated days for personnel to engage in wellness-oriented activities could have a lasting effect and become a preventative approach to sick time rather than a reactive approach.

These are the types of questions we, as leaders in the military and First Responder professions, must begin to ask ourselves. The answers are often readily available; the challenge lies in taking action. To create a healthier and more sustainable culture, we must adopt proven strategies from sports medicine and industrial psychology, reevaluate outdated practices such as harmful shift schedules, and commit to prioritizing the health and wellness of our personnel without compromising mission effectiveness.

By doing so, we can honor the selflessness that defines our professions while ensuring that those who serve have long, healthy lives beyond their careers. Also remember, it is essential to work together; Veterans, Law Enforcement, EMS and Fire, taking care of each other as a community. The time for change is now.

Staying Healthy as We Develop a Wellness Culture

Maintaining a healthy outlook and a healthy culture is essential, not just as Veterans and First Responders, but also as individuals. One of the most important ways to achieve this is by staying mentally organized and avoiding the buildup of emotional and psychological burdens.

A powerful analogy for this is a hoarder's house-one of the most dangerous environments in the event of a fire. A house filled with old, unnecessary items becomes a fire hazard, burning quickly and uncontrollably when disaster strikes. Similarly, our minds can become cluttered with past traumas, grudges, negative thoughts, and unhealthy patterns. If we don't actively cleanout these burdens through therapy, wellness practices, and self-reflection, we risk mental and emotional overload when life's inevitable challenges arise.

By cleaning out our mental clutter, we create space for clarity, resilience, and peace of mind. When a crisis occurs-our proverbial "fire"-we are better equipped to handle it without being consumed by the weight of unresolved struggles.

The second critical component of wellness is learning to repurpose hardships into motivation for growth. Life provides us with fuel in many forms-both positive and negative experiences. The way we choose to use that fuel determines whether it drives us forward or burns us down.

We can take our negative experiences and convert them into power-using them as motivation, wisdom, and guidance to help ourselves and others. Or, we can allow those experiences to accumulate like spilled gasoline, creating emotional hazards that make us vulnerable to destructive breakdowns. The choice is ours. By containing and repurposing the difficult things we've faced, we can use them to strengthen our character and purpose rather than allowing them to define us in a negative way.

It's also crucial to understand that none of this should be done alone. Seeking out others in our community, fellow

Veterans, First Responders, and individuals committed to healthy living, provides a reinforcing support network that fosters positive habits and mindsets.

Negativity spreads easily, and it's common in our line of work to encounter people who are cynical, burned out, or caught in destructive cycles. If we surround ourselves with that energy, we may start to mirror it ourselves. However, the same is true for positivity. When we align ourselves with healthy, motivated people, we naturally adopt more positive behaviors and perspectives.

This is the challenge: choose the right environment. Surround yourself with people who uplift, encourage, and challenge you in a healthy way-both personally and professionally. When we cultivate positive circles of influence, we begin to notice and appreciate the good in life, reinforcing our overall well-being.

Building a Sustainable Wellness Culture

The journey toward better mental, physical, and emotional health in the Veteran and First Responder communities is not just about individual change; it's about cultural change. While self-improvement is essential, real progress happens when entire communities embrace wellness as a shared value.

Several items are essential, as mentioned and hinted at several times in this book, within any First Responder Agency or Veterans group. These are front-end education/training, trained wellness, peers and advocates in the middle, and vetted/available resources for any wellness concern on the backend.

This shift must happen on two levels

1. Individual Responsibility – Every Veteran and First Responder must take ownership of their own wellness journey. This means being proactive about self-care, seeking support, and making health-conscious choices.

2. Organizational and Cultural Change – Leadership within our institutions must prioritize wellness, integrating it into training, policies, and everyday operations. This means advocating for better shift schedules, access to mental health resources, peer support networks, and leadership accountability when it comes to personnel well-being.

A sustainable wellness culture isn't just about reducing burnout and preventing suicides-though those are critical. It's about creating a future where First Responders and Veterans live long, fulfilling, and healthy lives well beyond their years of service.

For decades, many in our professions have operated under the silent struggle mentality-the idea that suffering in isolation is just "part of the job." This is an outdated and dangerous way of thinking. The reality is that our health and longevity matter just as much as the mission itself.

A sustainable wellness culture also means rejecting the stigma surrounding mental health care. Seeking help should be seen as a sign of strength, not weakness. Just as we wouldn't ignore a bullet wound or a broken leg, we should not ignore psychological injuries, chronic stress, or emotional exhaustion. The brain is just as vital as the body, and protecting our mental health is essential for long-term success.

Organizations should actively create peer support systems that encourage openness, connection, and shared solutions. A peer support culture doesn't mean venting about every bad day-it means creating structured, reliable, and judgment-free spaces where warriors can talk, listen, and support one another in meaningful ways.

The responsibility doesn't just fall on leadership. If you are a Veteran or First Responder reading this, ask yourself: What am I doing to contribute to a culture of wellness?

1. Do I check in on my peers?
2. Do I encourage healthy habits in my community?
3. Do I model good behavior when it comes to wellness and self-care?
4. Am I open about my own challenges, showing others that it's okay to seek help?
5. We can all be agents of change. A wellness culture starts with us.

Chris's Perspective

Advanced Life Support in the street began as an experiment with the Freedom House Ambulance Service in Pittsburgh, PA, circa 1967. Dr. Nancy Caroline and a group of dedicated African American men served their neighborhoods so effectively that affluent communities began requesting them. You had a much better chance of surviving in a Freedom House ambulance with real paramedics. They brought advanced life support to the street.

Despite their success, the first paramedics in the country were discarded after years of service, and for a long time, no one knew their story. Sadly, many paramedics are still discarded today.

EMS has come a long way since then, and in recent years, the Freedom House paramedics have finally received the recognition they deserved. Compared to nursing, law enforcement, the fire service, and the military, all of which have more tenure, structure, and support, paramedics are still relatively young as a profession. Thankfully, people are starting to notice, and the tide is turning. Post-pandemic, I feel our biggest supporters are those same public service partners. At least where I work, we're fortunate enough to be one big, dysfunctional public service family. I'm truly lucky and blessed.

I don't mean to open cynically or come off as pessimistic or jealous. We solve problems by first acknowledging the truth of the issues- and modern EMS has plenty we're actively working together to address. My name is Chris, and I'm just another paramedic riding the meat wagon. I've been in the mix since 2009. And while I have my moments, I'm committed to not hating this job. I still love people. They complicate things and make it hard sometimes-it is what it is. But I love my colleagues most of all. I also hate them sometimes because they won't let me be lazy or make excuses, no matter the circumstance. Together, we've worked hard to create a culture I'm proud of, and we're always pushing forward.

It's no secret that EMS has long been the redheaded stepchild of public service. I think that remains true in part because our own collective negativity keeps it alive. We've embraced the chip on our shoulder too much. I'd argue we often lead the public service world in bitterness and cynicism. And ironically, most paramedics would agree that much of the stress at work is caused by other paramedics-gossiping, bickering, fighting, and engaging in a bizarre competition we created ourselves. For what? Bragging rights? Accolades? Promotions? Meanwhile, other public servants look on, wondering why the hell we aren't just supporting each other.

It's not hard to understand why we are the way we are. Our role in the system is different. We're 100% responsible for the dead and dying. It's a performance metric. Society demands we shoulder that weight. We're the collective grief mop of the world, guaranteed to show up at your door in ten minutes or less.

Anyone in critical care knows how finite and fragile human life is. We lose a lot in this job. Sleep doesn't come easily.

Our role inherently breeds individualism, yet public service works best as a team. On most calls, a single paramedic makes all the health-related decisions. The highest level of care always bears the most liability. We're evaluated on every call. Each agency reviews charts, provides quality assurance, and encourages collaborative learning. Or at least, that's the goal.

Usually, we're two people making life-changing decisions with limited or unreliable information. And those decisions affect a patient for the rest of their life, whether that's 15 minutes or 55 years. That's a heavy burden.

The primary paramedic on a 911 call assumes command and responsibility for the scene. They must answer for everything that went wrong-or right.

As much as I love this job, it's gotten more dangerous. Paramedics are assaulted. Some have been murdered. Everyone I know in the field has been punched, kicked, or bitten at least once-usually on psychiatric or intoxicated calls. Some medics never make it to retirement, taken out by career-ending injuries.

Most systems have mixed-level ambulance crews. Only the best jobs staff dual ALS providers. So often, a 24-year-old with a one-year certification and two years of street experience is paired with a 20-year-old EMT-Basic-and we expect them to get it right all the time. I've met plenty of providers who've washed out of great jobs. While a lack of self-awareness can be a factor, I can't help but think we've set many of them up for failure.

Mistakes in EMS happen for many reasons-lack of training, exhaustion, dehydration, toxic leadership, and sleep deprivation top the list. Ironically, our own health as a profession is terrible. Many paramedics chain-smoke, vape, binge-eat, drink excessively, and struggle with obesity, substance abuse, and alcoholism.

How sharp are your clinical decisions after 36 hours and twelve calls when your baseline health is trash?

Sounds extreme, but it's happening everywhere, right now. We've been in a staffing crisis since I started. We keep showing up and doing our best. But we don't want pizza parties or hero tributes. We want to be paid appropriately, staffed properly, trained extensively, and respected as professionals. Our pay and benefits should at least match our counterparts in other public service fields.

It's getting better-I've seen it- but the pace is slow. So I stomp my feet and raise my voice. Here you go, Chris-here's the attention you ordered. Thanks!

Brooding, cathartic rambling aside- we've talked enough about the darker parts of EMS in 2025. The point here is growth and change. And in my opinion, it starts with culture. It begins with us- and ends with us-every day, always.

I don't think it's hard to support and encourage each other. But being an outspoken advocate for mental health and wellness? That can be soul-crushing. I need your help. Join my cult. I spent my youth peer pressuring people toward drugs and alcohol. Now I do the opposite.

Our average life expectancy as First Responders is 57. The deck is stacked against us from day one. We need to acknowledge the difficulty of this profession and recognize how our coping mechanisms often hurt more than they help.

We have families and loved ones depending on us. There's nothing noble about destroying your personal life for your professional one. That's a lie. Don't become a statistic. So-how do you cope?

We're all shaped by our experiences. Many of us don't even realize our self-destructive habits are coping mechanisms in disguise. Our job isn't normal-if there is such a thing. What we see, smell, touch, hear-and sometimes taste-is not normal. (Don't lick your gloves. But if you've stood in a room full of blood, you've tasted the iron in the air.)

We manage trauma, others' and our own, and that takes a toll. So sure, take a mental health day. Except that in the real world, an ambulance goes out of service. Our coworkers pick up the slack. Innocent people might suffer. Hard to enjoy your day off when you're weighed down with guilt.

Still, a good day at work, laughing with friends, pushing each other clinically, making the best of things, can do more than we realize. Dark humor is our go-to. I'm great at unhinged hilarity. But we must be careful-we can become the dark humor if we're not balanced.

Alcoholism is another coping mechanism, especially in blue-collar circles. The bar is the traditional place to unwind. But we need to move away from that. The data is in-it's not good. Alcohol raises cortisol and worsens stress. It's a false release. We need better outlets.

Some departments are even accepting medical marijuana use. I believe that every First Responder deserves access to every legitimate medication that can support their wellness. Research backs it up, but we must take a measured, physician-guided approach with any substance, including ketamine, psilocybin, and ibogaine. Alcohol's risks are clear. The long-term effects of marijuana and other substances still need study.

One of the biggest mental health topics is ironically physical fitness. We need to be fit to do this job, yet EMS ranks lowest in fitness among public services. Most departments lack agility requirements and rarely enforce the ones they have.

EMS: "Earn, Money, Sleeping." It's an old joke and our curse. A sedentary lifestyle should not be our cultural norm. The body and mind are connected. We need to move.

Everyone needs their fitness "thing." For me, it's Brazilian Jiu-Jitsu and Muay Thai. I'm obsessed. I could write ten more paragraphs about the benefits. Jiu-Jitsu is for everyone and could one day save your life.

It doesn't matter what it is. I have friends who run, hike, climb, CrossFit, swim, lift, dive-you name it. We need healthy outlets-not just to live longer but to stay sharp for our families, patients, and partners.

We should manage what we can control and manage our reactions to what we can't. We already do this. But we can all improve. Chaos gets thrown at us. We're expected to transmute it into something good.

With Ben's help, we've made the connection-individual, physical, and mental wellness are intertwined. They're all within our control. We perform best as a team. Silence kills us. Open dialogue, support, and resilience are essential. It's time to change.

So why aren't we all glowing, fit, sober, smiling, hand-holding people? EMS has a culture war. Being a train wreck is… cool. Everyone laughs. We laugh together-or behind each other's backs. Being unhinged makes you popular.

We need honest conversations. We can uplift and hold each other accountable-with compassion. Check in. Be obnoxious if needed. Mediate conflict. Don't fan the flames. Push people to talk and resolve their issues, not validate the drama.

We must learn to tell the difference between roasting and bullying. I love roasting-but when we cross the line, we hit people in ways that matter deeply. If my roast cuts too deep, say so. I thought we were goofing. I don't want anyone to feel awful.

Assume the best in each other. Much of our conflict stems from assumptions and posttraumatic stress. PTS accumulates. We need rest. We need decompression.

We're not going to win every time-but we can focus on small wins. We must respect our work and understand that without prioritizing ourselves, we can't be the people our families, patients, and coworkers need us to be. We must save ourselves if we're going to save others.

I'm on a mission-to make support, encouragement, resilience, fitness, sobriety, wellness, camaraderie, and compassionate accountability the norm in

EMS. Call me soft. I'll challenge that. It takes real courage to talk about this. It takes bravery to face our dysfunction. But we are stronger together. And we owe it to ourselves-and to those training now for this calling. Are you with me?

-Christopher Schierloh, Paramedic

Resources and Providers

An essential part of developing a wellness culture is cultivating quality resources alongside effective wellness techniques and practices. With this in mind, how are resources located, vetted, and made available?

The first and most obvious approach is to utilize what is already accessible-such as the VA for Veterans and EAP/Employee Health services for First Responders. These resources can provide a foundational backbone for a local wellness group. But is that all that's needed? Absolutely not.

Additional resources are critical for fostering a culture of healthy warriors. One of the most important is the development and availability of culturally competent mental health professionals. Ensuring cultural competence is essential, as we want therapists, psychiatrists, and other mental health providers to truly empathize with our work and culture, and offer the kind of support necessary for genuine growth and healing. Cognitive Behavioral Therapy (CBT) and Positive Psychology are both valuable approaches to consider. These therapeutic modalities help reframe perspectives, beginning the process of healing by shifting negative experiences into opportunities for growth.

The next pillar is physical wellness. While a gym membership or fitness program is helpful, it is not sufficient on its own. Are we teaching each other healthy exercise techniques, or are we promoting self-injurious practices? While completing the mission is important, we must ask ourselves: are we sacrificing our bodies between missions? Are we allowing ourselves the time to heal when injured? Are we scheduling physicals, screenings for cancer, and cardiovascular evaluations? These are essential questions to consider. Building relationships with physical therapists, chiropractors, internal medicine practitioners, yoga instructors, martial arts instructors, and others in the wellness space is vital to supporting long-term physical health.

We must also cultivate resources that support our families and financial wellbeing-two areas often neglected in the First Responder and Veteran communities. Are we ensuring that our children and spouses have access to support, or are we overlooking their needs, risking relationship breakdown and family neglect? Access to marriage counselors, couples retreats, children's play therapists, and other family-oriented professionals is essential.

Financial experts also play a key role. While focusing on retirement is ideal, the reality is that many of us have put financial planning on the "I'll get to it" list. Professionals who understand our fast-paced culture and can provide practical financial wellness tips and planning guidance can be invaluable.

Finally, we cannot overlook spiritual health. Whether through a local church, a Buddhist spiritual guide, or a self-help resource, we must encourage our brothers and sisters to cultivate a sense of purpose. A warrior without purpose often begins to spiral, with their sense of duty being the first to erode.

Even if someone is not religious, the fact that we swore an oath means we believe in something greater than ourselves. We must protect that belief system, whatever it may be, to prevent resentment from creeping in toward the society we've committed to protect.

Making these resources visible and easily accessible is key. One effective method is creating a regional guide with a comprehensive list of vetted resources. Contacting providers in advance to ensure they are open to working with nontraditional schedules and prioritizing timely access is crucial. Many First Responders wait too long to seek help-a two-month waiting list isn't useful in a moment of crisis.

Once resources are identified and accessible, maintaining those relationships and continuously sharing information is essential. Wellness isn't a one-time effort-it requires ongoing commitment. If you hear about a new gym opening nearby, check it out. If a new counseling office opens, visit or review their website. This ongoing engagement helps foster mutual support between our communities and those we serve.

It's important to remember: many people genuinely want to help-we just need to let them, and make sure our people know that support is available.

The Mission of Restoration

At its core, this book is about restoration. The world needs warriors-people who are willing to step into danger, protect the innocent, and make sacrifices for the greater good. But warriors, too, need protection-especially from the internal battles that can arise after years of service.

Restoration isn't about returning to who we were before service-it's about embracing who we are now and learning how to live full, meaningful, and healthy lives.

The numbers don't lie-First Responders and Veterans are at a significantly higher risk for suicide, chronic illness, and reduced life expectancy. But these numbers are not set in stone. We have the power to change them by choosing wellness, choosing connection, and choosing to support one another in the same way we do on the battlefield or in an emergency situation.

We must remember that our identity is not just defined by our profession. We are more than soldiers, officers, firefighters, and paramedics-we are people, friends, family members, mentors, and leaders. Our worth is not measured solely by what we have endured but by how we rise and restore ourselves in the aftermath.

This mission-the mission of restoration-is one that cannot be undertaken alone. We must continue to foster peer support, leadership accountability, and personal responsibility in wellness. We must build systems that help warriors heal, thrive, and live long, fulfilling lives.

It's time for a new approach-one that acknowledges the weight of our experiences while also championing the strength, resilience, and worth of every warrior who has ever served. Together, we can change the story for future generations of Veterans and First Responders.

Moving Forward: How You Can Take Action

Now that you've read this book, I encourage you to take action in a meaningful way. Here's how:

1. Apply What You've Learned – Start implementing wellness practices in your daily life. Whether it's checking in with peers, improving your physical health, or seeking therapy, small changes lead to lasting impact.
2. Spread Awareness – Share these insights with fellow Veterans and First Responders. Let them know that they are not alone and that a collaborative culture of wellness is possible in the overall warrior community of all of us.
3. Be a Leader in Change – Whether you're in an official leadership position or not, set an example. Model healthy behaviors and create space for others to do the same.

4. Seek and Offer Support – If you're struggling, reach out. If you see someone else struggling, don't wait, step in.
5. Advocate for Better Systems – Push for policies that prioritize mental and physical wellness in First Responder and Veteran communities.
6. Remember and practice the three-tiered approach for our Veteran and First Responder organizations.
    a. Educating and training about wellness and healthier living.
    b. Peers and advocates within our organizations and community to usher along change.
    c. Culturally competent and available provider resources readily available for our people.

Thank you for reading, for serving, and for taking the first steps toward a healthier, more connected, and more resilient future. The choice is ours, and the time for it is now!

Take Action to Change the Culture: Posttraumatic Growth Groups

An essential part of the mission to restore warriors has emerged through the work we have done since the inception of our local wellness team and the publication of the first edition of this book. Camaraderie and purpose-driven growth have proven to be highly effective in helping Veterans and First Responders begin the important mission of wellness.

Some of the most meaningful growth we have witnessed within the Veteran and First Responder community has come from those who attend our weekly Posttraumatic Growth meetings. These gatherings build on the teachings of Dr. Richard Tedeschi, many of which are reflected in Restoring the Warrior and Struggle Well. Both are recommended readings for anyone interested in creating a group.

These meetings foster shared strength, communal purpose, and the reminder that none of us struggle alone. We believe these groups can be effective anywhere in the country, provided they follow the same mission and guiding principles that have shaped our local groups.

Creating these groups is straightforward. Each of our groups began with three to five motivated Veterans and First Responders who shared a common mission, and from there they grew.

We have named our local groups Tribe of the Restored Warriors meetings, though attendees often refer to them simply as The Tribe or Restored Warriors. You are welcome to use this name and logo, or to create your own local group identity and name, but please stay true to the principles and format outlined in this guide, as they have been heavily researched and tested to protect confidentiality and create a safe space that fosters growth within the warrior community.

These meetings provide a safe community in which to practice growth and thriving within the warrior community. In many ways, they function much like a workout group, yoga club, or recovery group, offering a consistent space where people can come together, strengthen themselves, support one another, and continue moving forward.

The following is our Posttraumatic Growth meeting guide, made freely available to the warrior community to support the creation and operation of Posttraumatic Growth meetings.

Digital Copy of the Posttraumatic Growth Group Meeting Guide

For a free digital copy of this meeting guide, please go to:

https://bticonsultingservice.com/torw

Or scan the QR code below

Restoring the Warrior 2nd ed.

POSTTRAUMATIC GROWTH (PTG) GROUP

Meeting Guide & Facilitator Manual

Version 04/2026

Permission to Duplicate and Share

The framework, structure, language, and materials contained in this manual are derived from the book *Restoring the Warrior: A Guide to Veteran and First Responder Wellness*, authored by Dr. Benjamin Iobst.

This model represents an applied adaptation of the principles, research, and wellness philosophy presented in Restoring the Warrior, translated into a structured, peer-led weekly PTG meeting format.

This manual constitutes a derivative work of Restoring the Warrior, created to expand access to peer-led PTG communities.

The following materials may be freely photocopied, replicated, and distributed solely for the purpose of starting or operating a PTG Group.

• The PTG Meeting Manual

• The 12 Guiding Principles

• Facilitator Guidance

• Weekly Reflection Framework

• Closing Statement and Group Pledge

By using these materials, you agree to:

1. Preserve the meaning, integrity, and intent of the Guiding Principles.

2. Maintain peer-led, volunteer facilitation.

3. Provide access free of charge.

4. Never monetize meetings.

5. Protect confidentiality as non-negotiable.

6. Avoid altering core language in a manner that changes the spirit of the model.

7. Clearly identify the material as derived from Restoring the Warrior when redistributed in substantial form.

These materials are shared so that any Veteran or First Responder may benefit anywhere, at any time.

Dr. Benjamin Iobst
US Army Combat Veteran
Retired Law Enforcement Officer
Author, Restoring the Warrior

Independent Status, Assumption of Risk, and Limitation of Liability

Each PTG Group is an independent, locally organized, peer-led, non-clinical community gathering. Unless specifically stated in a separate written agreement signed by the applicable party, no PTG Group is owned, operated, managed, supervised, controlled, insured, or clinically overseen by Boulder Crest Foundation, Dr. Benjamin Iobst, BTI Consulting Service LLC, or any contributing author.

References to Boulder Crest Foundation, Dr. Benjamin Iobst, BTI Consulting Service LLC, contributing authors, Restoring the Warrior, Warrior PATHH, Struggle Well, Tribe of the Restored Warriors, or related materials, concepts, or teachings are provided for educational, inspirational, or informational purposes only. Such references reflect shared principles, educational influence, or permitted use of materials, and do not create any ownership interest, agency relationship, employment relationship, partnership, joint venture, fiduciary duty, supervisory duty, clinical duty, or assumption of responsibility for any local PTG Group, facilitator, host site, volunteer, participant, or event.

Each local PTG Group, facilitator, organizer, and host site remains solely responsible for its own operations, screening practices, conduct, safety procedures, referrals, confidentiality practices, legal compliance, and response to any participant issue, emergency, or crisis.

To the fullest extent permitted by law, Boulder Crest Foundation, Dr. Benjamin Iobst, BTI Consulting Service LLC, and any contributing author disclaim and assume no liability for any claim, injury, death, loss, damage, cost, or expense arising out of or related to any local PTG Group or any person's attendance at, participation in, facilitation of, organization of, hosting of, reliance on, or connection with such group. This includes, but is not limited to, any act, omission, statement, referral decision, failure to refer, failure to obtain treatment, failure to respond to crisis, breach of confidentiality by others, emotional distress, interpersonal conflict, or the conduct of any participant, facilitator, volunteer, host, or third party.

Participation in any PTG Group is voluntary and at the participant's own risk. No representation or guarantee is made regarding safety, suitability, confidentiality, supervision, or outcomes. Nothing in this document creates, or shall be interpreted to create, any duty of care, protective duty, clinical duty, or ongoing obligation on the part of Boulder Crest Foundation, Dr. Benjamin Iobst, BTI Consulting Service LLC, or any contributing author.

Introduction

Posttraumatic Growth (PTG) Groups exist to give Veterans and First Responders a place to continue growing together in community. Rooted in the principles of Posttraumatic Growth, these groups are designed to help participants turn pain into purpose, replace isolation with connection, strengthen identity through shared experience, and continue practicing growth on a regular basis.

The format used for these groups is based on the Tribe of the Restored Warriors (TORW) model, a peer-led, non-clinical framework created to bring the principles of Posttraumatic Growth into ongoing local community practice. The TORW model is derived from the teachings, principles, and guidance found in *Restoring the Warrior: A Guide to Veteran and First Responder Wellness* and was developed to help carry forward and reinforce the transformational work introduced through posttraumatic growth programs such as Warrior PATHH and Struggle Well offered by the Boulder Crest Foundation.

This PTG group format is informed in part by the Posttraumatic Growth framework advanced by the Boulder Crest Foundation and is built around the same foundational principles of growth through struggle. Boulder Crest is a nationally recognized nonprofit organization serving Veterans, First Responders, and their families through the science and application of Posttraumatic Growth. The TORW-based format adapts those principles into a peer-led, non-clinical group model focused on connection, meaning-making, resilience, and sustained personal growth following adversity.

These groups are peer-led, volunteer-facilitated, free of charge, hosted in donated spaces, and centered on growth rather than clinical treatment. They are not therapy, not crisis response, and not a replacement for professional care. They are communities of warriors committed to growth.

Shared Vision, Independent Structure

These PTG Groups are built around a shared vision of growth through struggle, meaning-making, connection, and continued personal development following adversity. While they follow a common format and guiding principles, each local group remains independent in its structure, leadership, and operation.

This shared vision reflects alignment around core Posttraumatic Growth concepts and the purpose of creating peer-led, growth-centered spaces for Veterans, First Responders, and others with shared lived experience. It does not imply outside ownership, governance, clinical oversight, operational control, supervision, insurance coverage, or assumption of liability by any external organization.

Each PTG Group:

- Operates independently at the local level
- Is peer-led and volunteer-facilitated
- Is hosted in donated community spaces
- Remains free of charge
- Is not a clinical program
- Does not provide therapy, diagnosis, or medical treatment

Local facilitators and participants are responsible for:

- Adhering to the 12 Guiding Principles
- Maintaining confidentiality
- Preserving the non-clinical structure
- Ensuring meetings remain growth-centered
- Following appropriate crisis referral procedures when necessary

Shared vision creates alignment.
Independent structure preserves integrity.
Local ownership supports sustainability.

The Tribe of the Restored Warriors Model

The Tribe of the Restored Warriors Model was developed in Pennsylvania as a structured format for weekly Posttraumatic Growth meetings inspired by the principles and framework in *Restoring the Warrior*. It was created to give Veterans, First Responders, and approved supporters a consistent, peer-led space where people can come together, support one another, and continue growing through life's struggles.

The original Pennsylvania meetings model emerged from a shared vision centered on Posttraumatic Growth and a community-based, growth-oriented approach to healing and transformation. The founding groups used the name *Tribe of the Restored Warriors*, reflecting the importance of connection, shared identity, and the process of growing stronger together.

As the model expands, each region or group may choose a locally meaningful name that fits its own community, culture, and identity. That flexibility allows each group to feel rooted in the people it serves while still staying connected to the larger PTG framework.

No matter what name is used, all PTG Groups must keep the core parts of the model in place, including:

- The 12 Guiding Principles
- The peer-led structure
- The volunteer model
- The free-access format
- The growth-centered mission
- Confidentiality standards

These pieces are what keep the model consistent, safe, accessible, and true to its purpose. So while the name can be adapted to fit the local community, the heart of the model stays the same.

The name may adapt locally. The principles do not.

12 Guiding Principles of Posttraumatic Growth Groups

1. **Our common purpose is to support one another in Posttraumatic growth by transforming pain into meaning and purpose.**
   We gather not to relive trauma but to reclaim strength and identity in the aftermath.
2. **Our group unity depends on mutual respect, shared experience, and a commitment to healing, not hierarchy.**
   Leadership may guide, but all voices are equal in the circle.
3. **The only requirement for participation is being a current or former Veteran or First Responder seeking growth after trauma.**
   All are welcome who share the mission.
4. **Each group should remain autonomous except in matters affecting the broader PTG community or violating group safety and values.**
   Groups should preserve the core format while adapting to local needs.
5. **Our group has one primary purpose: to help Veterans and First Responders heal through connection, growth, and shared mission.**
   We are not a therapy group; we are a tribe with a shared journey.
6. **We do not endorse or oppose any outside organization, political view, or religious belief.**
   Our strength lies in shared humanity, not ideology.
7. **Our groups are peer-led and non-clinical by design. Any professional involvement should be in support of, not in charge of, the group's mission.**
   We are not patients, we are warriors walking together.
8. **Posttraumatic growth is guided by the principles of shared stories, mutual support, and honoring each person's path.**
   Advice is offered only when invited. Judgment is never welcome.

9. **The group spirit is maintained by mutual accountability, adherence to group rules, and respect for the space and time of others.**
   We show up, we share space, we grow together.
10. **Our anonymity creates safety; what is shared in the group stays in the group.**
    Confidentiality is non-negotiable.
11. **Groups are facilitated by volunteers and hosted in donated spaces. No individual, agency, or organization owns the group. Participation is always free, and meetings may never be monetized.**
    This mission is built on service, not profit, carried forward by warriors for warriors.
12. **Our mission is to carry the message of healing and Posttraumatic growth to every Veteran and First Responder still suffering.**
    Each of us is proof that something beautiful can rise from what was broken.

How to Create a Group

1. Gather Committed Core Members

Every PTG Group begins with a small, committed core. Ideally, this includes three to five Veterans or First Responders willing to meet consistently and protect the mission of the group.

Before launching:

- Ensure all core members understand that the purpose of the group is Posttraumatic growth — not therapy.
- Confirm commitment to confidentiality.
- Establish agreement on growth-centered dialogue.
- Clarify that meetings are always free and volunteer-led.

Start small. Build consistency first. Culture grows from commitment.

2. Review the Meeting Guide

All core members should review the complete PTG Meeting Guide together to ensure philosophical and structural alignment before the first meeting.

During this review:

- Discuss the founding principles.
- Clarify boundaries and non-negotiables.
- Review higher-risk situation protocols.
- Confirm understanding of crisis referral procedures.

Alignment at the beginning protects integrity long-term.

3. Secure a Donated Space

PTG Groups operate in donated spaces to preserve independence, accessibility, and sustainability. A consistent meeting location builds psychological safety and reinforces group culture.

The location should be:

- Private
- Quiet
- Reliable week-to-week
- Free of charge
- Conducive to open, confidential conversation

Chairs should be arranged in a circle or open arrangement (U or Box) to reinforce equal voice and shared ownership.

Common examples of appropriate donated spaces include:

- Churches or faith-based community centers
- Union halls
- Police, fire, or EMS departmental training rooms
- Veterans associations (VFW, American Legion, etc.)
- Community centers
- Municipal buildings
- College or university classrooms
- Nonprofit organization meeting rooms

The space does not need to be elaborate. Consistency is more important than aesthetics.

Stability builds trust. Trust builds culture. Culture sustains growth.

4. Set a Weekly Time

Select a consistent day and time for weekly meetings. Repetition builds rhythm. Rhythm builds culture.

Once established, communicate clearly with members and maintain consistency whenever possible. Regular meeting cadence reinforces accountability and trust.

Facilitators of PTG Groups

Facilitators lead Posttraumatic Growth (PTG) meetings operating under the Tribe of the Restored Warriors Model. They are not "in charge" in a hierarchical sense and do not function as clinicians. They are culture stewards responsible for protecting the mission, structure, and integrity of the group. The group belongs to the collective.

The facilitator's role is to guide the meeting, maintain psychological safety, and ensure dialogue remains aligned with Posttraumatic growth principles.

Core Requirement

Facilitators must be current or former Veterans or First Responders who are committed to growth, confidentiality, and equal voice.

Strongly Recommended Background (Not Required)

- At least 6 months of participation in a PTG group
- Graduate of Warrior PATHH or Struggle Well
- Peer Support certification
- CIT (Crisis Intervention Team) training
- ICISF / CISM training
- Veteran or Military Peer Support training
- Trauma-informed training or relevant academic background

Facilitator Qualities

- Emotional regulation under stress
- Ability to redirect trauma loops toward meaning-making
- Commitment to equal voice and respectful dialogue

• Willingness to gently interrupt when needed to protect the mission

• Clear understanding that this is growth work — not therapy

• Commitment to confidentiality as sacred

Facilitator Responsibilities

• Open and close the meeting and maintain time boundaries

• Reinforce confidentiality and equal voice

• Review ground rules and keep the meeting growth-centered

• Redirect trauma dumping / war stories toward growth and meaning

• Prevent domination of airtime (use structured rounds when needed)

• Interrupt political/ideological drift and re-center the mission

• Monitor for emotional distress and initiate referral to external resources when needed

• Protect the 12 Guiding Principles and the non-clinical boundary of the group

Managing Common Challenges

- If a participant becomes stuck in trauma narration, redirect toward lessons learned, strength discovered, and meaning constructed.
- If attendance drops, facilitators should conduct personal outreach and reinforce consistency.
- If mission drift occurs, revisit the 12 Guiding Principles. Protecting the mission protects the group.

Higher-Risk Situations (Non-Clinical Referral)

These meetings are not therapy or crisis response. If any of the following arise, facilitators should refer externally and ensure the member is connected to appropriate support:

- Suicidal or homicidal ideation
- Severe emotional dysregulation or crisis needs
- Active substance instability/crisis
- Any situation where clinical intervention is clearly needed

Facilitator Sustainability

Facilitator burnout is real. Rotate leadership when possible, share responsibilities, and protect your own growth. Boundaries protect sustainability.

PTG Group Meeting Guide

Duration: 60 to 90 Minutes (depending on group size)

Purpose: To provide Veterans and First Responders with a safe, supportive environment to explore Posttraumatic Growth (PTG). Adaptations are allowed as long as the group's founding principles are respected.

Note: Groups are volunteer-led, held in donated spaces, and always free of charge. No individual or organization owns the group; it belongs to the collective.

Before the Meeting

- Set up chairs in a circle or similar arrangement to promote connection.
- Have the weekly reflection or reading ready.
- Keep the Closing Statement and Tribe Pledge available to read.

Step 1: Welcome the Group

Facilitator Reads:

"This is a closed Veterans and First Responders Posttraumatic Growth group. Attendance is limited to Military Veterans and First Responders, both current and former, as well as select supporters approved by the group.

The purpose of this group is to find purpose in our struggles, sharing each other's joys, perspectives, and triumphs in the aftermath of trauma. Please keep shares focused on growth, not on being stuck in trauma.

Please do not share who attends or what is discussed outside of this meeting. If you are struggling, please let us know so we can help.

Keep up the good fight!"

Step 2: Review Group Rules

- Avoid cross-talk or giving advice unless asked.
- Share your own experiences; your story has value.
- Avoid political discussions.
- Rank and roles are left at the door.
- Harsh language is acceptable but never directed at one another.
- Do not encourage self-destructive behaviors.
- Arrive on time when possible.

Step 3: Introductions

- If no new members are present: skip.
- If new members are present:

Veterans/First Responders: State your name and how you served.

Supporters: State your name and reason for attending. (If not appropriate, kindly ask them to leave.)

Step 4: Opening Discussion

Ask: "Does anyone have a growth challenge or reflection from this week they'd like to talk about today?"

• Allow space for brief check ins.

• Members share by first giving their first name, then their thoughts

Groups may incorporate a brief grounding practice, meditation practice or educational segment into opening discussion if they choose.

Step 5: Main Meeting Format

Choose one type of meeting (rotate weekly, group vote, or facilitator's choice):

Option A: Weekly Reflection Meeting

Note: Weekly reflections may come from the official weekly reflection list or a member's PTG-based reflection of the week. Keep shares focused on meaning-making and growth, not graphic detail or trauma processing.

Pick a reflection (by week of the year or random number 1–52).

Read it aloud.

Members share their reflections.

• Each begins by stating their first name, then their thoughts.

Facilitator: Redirect if the discussion becomes stuck in negativity, drifts into war stories, or loses focus.

Option B: Reading Meeting

Read a short excerpt from a PTG-focused book (e.g., Struggle Well, Restoring the Warrior, Transformed by Trauma).

Members share their reflections.

• Each begins by stating their first name, then their thoughts.

Facilitator: Use gentle redirection if the discussion strays.

Option C: Topic Meeting

Pick a topic that relates to PTG such as, increased personal strength, new possibilities, deeper relationships, appreciation for life, existential change.

Members share their thoughts and experiences around this topic.

• Each begins by stating their first name, then their thoughts.

Facilitator: Redirect if discussion becomes stuck in negativity, drifts into war stories, or loses focus.

Note: These are examples of meeting types, others may be used if it adheres to the guiding principles.

Step 6: Closing the Meeting

Begin the closing 10 to 15 minutes before the meeting ends.

1. Gratitude and Self Care Round

Each member shares:

- One thing they are grateful for today
- One thing they will do for self care

2. Facilitator Reads Closing Statement

"As we close today's meeting, let us remember why we come together. This group is not meant to replace any other program or clinical approach. It is here to give us space to grow, to support one another, and to remain open to many different paths of healing and recovery.

We carry forward the lessons of the Five Domains of Posttraumatic Growth:

- To find new appreciation in the small moments of life.
- To strengthen relationships through empathy, compassion, and connection.
- To discover new possibilities and directions we may not have seen before.
- To recognize the strength and courage we already hold within.
- To seek deeper meaning, whether through reflection, faith, or a renewed worldview.

Before anyone leaves, please make sure no one is in distress. If you notice a brother or sister struggling, check in and remind them that they are not alone. Together we can guide and encourage one another as we grow side by side.

Finally, let the work of this group extend beyond these walls. Stay connected, encourage one another, and live out growth with resilience, courage, and hope."

3. Tribe of the Restored Warriors Pledge

(Stand in a circle. Facilitator says, "Repeat after me," then recite together):

We are warriors; we are not meant to struggle alone.

I will face the past and the present with my Tribe.

Our mission is to heal and grow with intent and purpose.

Not just to survive but to thrive.

Weekly Reflections

These reflections were written by Veterans and First Responders who have experienced trauma, pursued Posttraumatic growth, and worked toward building meaning and purpose in its aftermath. The words reflect their lived experience and personal journey.

PTG Groups operating under this model are non-religious and do not promote any single belief system. While the meetings remain growth-centered and inclusive of all perspectives, some contributors reference spiritual practices, faith traditions, or personal belief systems that were meaningful in their individual growth process. Such references are personal expressions of experience, not endorsements of any ideology.

The purpose of these reflections is to encourage meaning-making, connection, forward movement, and continued growth.

They are not intended for trauma processing, but for growth-centered discussion.

Weekly Reflections by:

Bethany Adams, Law Enforcement Officer
Jennifer Aleman, US Army Combat Veteran (War on Terror)
David Alercia, USMC Veteran, Retired Law Enforcement Officer
William Carver, Paramedic, Former Firefighter
Thomas J. Carson, US Air Force Veteran
Chuck Durback, US Army Combat Veteran (Vietnam War)
Jeremy Gann, US Army Veteran (Iraq and Afghanistan War)
Christopher Hendricks, Law Enforcement Officer, Paramedic
John Hill, USMC Combat Veteran (Desert Storm), Retired Law Enforcement Officer
Dr. Benjamin Iobst, US Army Combat Veteran (Iraq War) and Retired Law Enforcement Officer
Amy J. Iobst, EMT
Jason Kesack, Law Enforcement Officer
John Kukitz, US Army Combat Veteran (Vietnam War)
James LaFey, US Air Force Veteran (Iraq and Afghanistan Wars)
Nate Laskey, USMC Combat Veteran (Iraq War)
Kevin McCloud, US Army Veteran
Kate Murray, Law Enforcement Officer
Adam Perreault, US Navy Veteran, Professional Firefighter
Freddie Reed, US Army Combat Veteran (Iraq War)
Dr. Thomas Ritter, US Army Veteran, Retired Law Enforcement Officer
Matthew Rush, Retired Law Enforcement Officer
Brian Sabo, Former Law Enforcement Officer
Shane Schmeckenbecher, US Army Combat Veteran (Iraq War), Probation Officer
Christopher Schierloh, Paramedic
Kenny Seagraves, US Navy Veteran
Robert Smith, US Army Combat Veteran (Desert Storm and Iraq War)
Trevor Tasetano, USMC Combat Veteran (Iraq War), Former Volunteer Firefighter
Drew Taylor, Probation Officer
John Turoczi, Retired Law Enforcement Officer
Justin Wright, USMC Combat Veteran (Iraq War)

1. **Growth does not mean the trauma was good, it means you were strong enough to create something meaningful after it.**

When I returned home from the Iraq War, I felt lost and directionless, carrying a head full of painful memories. I thought becoming a police officer would immediately give me purpose, only to discover that more trauma was waiting for me in that role. After several years of pushing through and beating myself up, both mentally and physically, my world eventually collapsed. In that collapse, I began opening up and sharing with other Veterans and First Responders as my true self, rather than staying armored. This openness created a sense of common purpose, not just to survive but to thrive, and I wanted the same for others walking this path with me.

Today, I still face struggles, but I see them as fuel to keep moving forward rather than reasons to remain stuck. What began as a personal battle has grown into a large community of people supporting one another. Without that original trauma, none of this would have been possible. I have learned to value even the worst experiences because it all comes down to perspective.

Dr. Benjamin Iobst, US Army Combat Veteran (Iraq War) and Law Enforcement Officer

2. You are not what happened to you; you are what you choose to build from it.

Every experience, good or bad, shapes us. Throughout my life, I have faced many challenges. One began when I was a child, before the chickenpox vaccine existed. I first contracted chickenpox, then developed mononucleosis from a weakened immune system. That led to encephalitis, swelling of the brain, and acute cerebellitis, which inflamed the cerebellum. These illnesses affected my coordination and caused partial paralysis on the left side of my body.

I refused to let a doctor's prognosis decide whether I would regain functionality. Instead, I chose to defy the odds and use that challenge as fuel, determined to prove them wrong. Over time, I regained nearly full functionality, went on to become a collegiate athlete for two years, enjoyed sports as hobbies, and later began my career as a police officer.

Through this and many other challenges, I learned that no event, even a traumatic one, has to define your life. What defines you is the ability to rise from the darkness and use it as an opportunity for growth.

One of my favorite quotes by Bernice Johnson Reagon captures this perfectly: "Life's challenges are not supposed to paralyze you, they're supposed to help you discover who you are." Hard events do not incapacitate us; they reveal what truly matters, the strengths we carry, the values we hold, and the resilience within us.

Bethany Adams, Law Enforcement Officer

3. Sometimes, the cracks in us are where the light begins to grow.

When I first began my journey, my fiancé gave me a "Beautifully Broken" necklace. The idea behind it was a reminder to let go of the illusion of perfection. I am not perfect, I am real. It encouraged me to accept my flaws, allow mistakes, and understand that I will not always have it all together.

At first, a crack may feel like damage, an imperfection that makes us weaker or less whole. We often try to hide it, to smooth over the jagged edges so no one sees the brokenness inside. But life shows us that cracks are not the end of our story; they are often where healing begins. Just as light seeps through a break in a wall, hope, wisdom, and compassion can emerge from the fractures in our hearts. Pain creates spaces that joy alone could never carve, making room for something new to grow.

These cracks are not signs of failure but proof of resilience. They reveal that we have endured, that the weight of life pressed hard but did not crush us. Through them, we see with greater depth and grace. What once felt like weakness becomes a passage for growth, connection, and even beauty. The light that shines through our scars transforms them into something sacred: reminders that brokenness can be a beginning, not an ending.

Kate Murray, Law Enforcement Officer

4. Pain can shatter us or shape us. PTG is the art of choosing the latter.

I have spent years walking into chaos so others did not have to. Before I wore the badge, I sat in therapy rooms, holding space for pain that was not mine. Later, the uniform became my armor. But no matter what role I filled, I carried a deeper weight: the trauma that shattered my world the day I lost my son to cancer.

People tried to comfort me with words like "He is in a better place" or "Everything happens for a reason." I would nod, but deep down I knew some pain does not come with a reason, and some losses will never be good. What I have come to understand is this: the trauma did not destroy me. It transformed me.

In the quiet after the funeral, I turned to pen and prayer. I surrounded myself with others who had also been through fire; warriors, responders, people just trying to hold themselves together. I let my pain make space for theirs. And somehow, out of heartbreak, I built something meaningful: a place where struggle was not weakness, where tears did not need to be hidden, and where healing did not mean forgetting.

My son's memory became more than grief; it became my mission. The wound is still there, and it probably always will be. But over time, it became the place where light could break through. Growth did not mean the trauma was good. It meant I was strong enough to create something that mattered from it. Not because the past was kind, but because I chose to be.

Jason Kesack, Law Enforcement Officer

5. Healing doesn't mean forgetting; it means carrying the memory differently.

Throughout my life and career, I have faced challenges and experiences that make me press "Pause" so I can process what just happened. Those pauses are mental stutter steps that help me make sense of an abnormal experience so I can move forward. I press "Pause" to allow myself to catch up, but it does not pause the memory, which continues.

I pressed Pause several times in my teenage years, then a few more times when I was in the Navy, and I continue to press Pause as a firefighter. Pressing Pause temporarily interrupts the movie, but it also takes away from the enjoyment and quality of the production.

When you watch a movie and press Pause to better understand a complex scene, it does not end the movie; it is just an interruption. Traumatic experiences in our lives are interruptions, some longer than others, and often very complex. We will never forget them, but we press play and keep enjoying the rest of the movie.

Adam Perreault, US Navy Veteran and Professional Firefighter

6. Growth sometimes begins in the most difficult places.

For me, it came through loss and an unexpected lesson in letting go.

A few years ago, my mentor passed away from cancer. After his passing, I was not familiar with how to grieve. I shut myself off from the world again and suffered in silence. After two years of this, I attended a bonfire where you write what you want to be free of on a paint stick and toss it into the fire. There were also rocks, or "strength rocks," with different inspiring messages on them.

I grabbed one of the rocks without looking at it and went back by the fire. I started to overthink what the "strength rock" was for. "Does it need to be something I need help with, or is it something I'm already decent at doing?" I thought. So I went back to where the rocks were and ran into the lady running the event. I asked her, "Do I need the rock to mean I'm good in this area, or that I need help in this area?" She said, "We do that, don't we? We overthink everything. You should just let go."

She asked what my rock said, and I pulled it out. Written on the rock were the words: "Let go."

This began my ability to heal and to let go-not forgetting the memories of my mentor or the lessons he gave me, but letting go of the suffering attached to his passing. Years after this experience, I have found peace with Wilson's death and learned to truly let go.

Justin Wright, USMC Combat Veteran (Iraq War)

7. Even in the ashes of loss, new values and deeper gratitude can rise.

Even in the ashes of loss, new values and deeper gratitude can rise, but only through work. For me, work became a lifeline. I wrestled with addiction and alcoholism for years, never fully losing function but never truly living. I was swollen, sick, and absent, especially as a father. Sobriety brought clarity, and with it, the epiphanies began. I got back on the mat, reclaimed my health, and even endured divorce with steady and sober resolve.

I struggle every day, but I struggle well. I am blessed to work in a culture of peers who understand the weight of our calling, advocate for EMS as a profession, and uphold the highest standards for themselves and for our industry. That support has made all the difference.

I remain a work in progress, but I improve daily. More importantly, I have learned the power of connection. When we unite for a mission or purpose, our resilience is unmatched. Through years of disaster, we have responded, rescued, and rebuilt together. It is time to bring that same strength inward. Just as our law enforcement, fire, and military colleagues have, EMS must invest in wellness and resilience.

The tides are turning. Change is slow in some places, but many EMS systems are beginning to evolve. Together, we can build a culture grounded in wellness, one where we learn to carry each other's burdens. In unity, we will not only struggle well, but we will struggle less, and in doing so, ensure a brighter future for ourselves and those we serve.

Christopher Schierloh, Paramedic

8. Trauma writes a chapter, not the whole book.

Trauma writes a chapter, and some of those chapters are hard to read. But trauma does not write the whole book.

We once had two officers ambushed during a domestic call. When asked if weapons were present, the wife answered, "I don't know." That vague response raised their instincts. As the first officer entered, he heard the charging handle of an AR slam forward and dove for cover. Both officers survived with only minor shrapnel injuries.

A few days later, I responded to a stabbing in progress. Another officer and I went upstairs and knocked, but no one answered. Both cars were outside, child seats still inside. Anxiety rose as I thought of the earlier ambush. We made entry and found her dead. We found him too, and I used my Taser instead of my firearm.

For weeks I carried guilt, believing we could have saved her. The medical examiner's report later showed she was killed about 14 seconds before our first knock. That truth helped, but what helped more were the buddy checks-calls and texts from friends who would not give up on me. At first, I was too shut down to notice, but they kept trying until they broke through.

That is my guidance: keep trying. Let those who suffer in silence know they matter. That moment did not define me, but it gave me brothers I will carry with me forever.

John Hill, USMC Combat Veteran (Desert Storm), Retired Law Enforcement Officer

9. Your survival was the first miracle; what you do with it is the second.

After two tours in Iraq with a combat engineer company in the Marine Corps, I came home, but I wasn't really home. The war followed me. I carried the sights, the sounds, and the ghosts everywhere I went. I didn't deal with it. I drowned it. I self-medicated, I blew up relationships, and I isolated until I was damn near gone.

That's the dark side of survival. You're breathing, but you're not living.

The second miracle came when I finally reached out. I walked into a Veterans group and found guys who had lived the same nightmares. They showed me that strength isn't hiding it-it's owning it. It's facing the demons head-on with brothers and sisters who refuse to let you fall.

Your survival means you still have a chance. The struggles don't define the rest of your life. What you choose to do with that survival does. There's a second miracle waiting, and it begins the moment you take that first step out of isolation and into connection.

Nate Laskey, USMC Combat Veteran (Iraq War)

10. Growth is not linear; it's often a journey of hills and valleys.

Ever since I was young, I remember how easily I became frustrated when things did not go my way. Whether it was underperforming at a karate tournament or not earning the test scores I wanted, those feelings of disappointment carried into adulthood.

Over time, I learned something important. If I excelled at everything all the time, I would become bored and complacent, and in my line of work, complacency can be deadly. Struggle forces us to adjust, adapt, and grow. When things do not go your way, you can give up, dwell on the setback, or take a step back to understand what it is you truly want to achieve.

Sometimes going from point A to point B is not the best path. Maybe you need to go from A to C first. Now you have options. You can circle back to B if it still matters, or continue to D if that is the stronger path forward. What once felt like failure becomes part of the map, not the end of the journey.

Life rarely unfolds in a straight line. It is the detours, challenges, and alternate routes that teach us resilience and creativity. In the end, success is not about everything going perfectly, but about continuing to move forward with purpose.

Trevor Tasetano, USMC Combat Veteran (Iraq War), Former Firefighter

11. Some lessons can only be learned in the aftermath.

After a mission went bad, my weapons specialist and my friend took his own life. He was under the care of professionals who promised to meet his needs and keep him safe. I took a voluntary temporary duty assignment, and when I came back weeks later, he was gone. No goodbye, no send off, not even a final act of sacrifice that others could hold on to. Just gone.

I spent more than a decade blaming myself for not being there. To support, to protect, to watch his six, or simply to hold his hand at the end. The guilt weighed heavily, as though I had failed him.

In time, I came to understand that it was not my choice to make. No matter how much I would have moved mountains to save him, the decision was his. I did not abandon him. He knew he could lean on me in any capacity. Nothing I could have done would have changed what happened, because it was not mine to decide.

Growth came only when I accepted that we are each the arbiters of our own journeys. The most we can do is offer a hand, be present, and show we care. It is up to them to take it. That was a hard lesson, but an essential one.

James Lafey, US Air Force Combat Veteran (Iraq and Afghanistan Wars)

12. Posttraumatic growth is not bouncing back-it's rebuilding forward.

For a long time, isolation felt comfortable until it did not. Being alone felt safe, but I was stuck in negative thinking, trapped in a constant loop of self-defeating thoughts and actions. That cycle kept me small and disconnected.

Everything began to change when I found a group of healthy Veterans. For the first time, I had a tribe I could lean on and share my thoughts with. Talking things through helped quiet the negative self-talk and gave me a clearer perspective.

Now I spend at least three to five days each week either talking with or spending time alongside these men and women. Together, we remind each other of truths that are easy to forget when you are alone. As the saying goes, you cannot see the forest through the trees, but someone else can see it for you.

Justin Wright, USMC Combat Veteran (Iraq War)

13. Strength isn't the absence of pain-it's continuing to love, trust, and serve despite it.

As Veterans and First Responders, we know pain is not just physical. It is the memories that weigh heavily, the moments that replay in the quiet hours, the losses that time does not erase. Sometimes the world tells us that being strong means never showing weakness, never admitting the hurt. But in God's eyes, strength looks different.

True strength is found when we choose to keep our hearts open despite the risk of being wounded again. It is trusting that God is still present when our circumstances feel overwhelming. It is showing up to serve, even when we feel emptied out.

Jesus Himself walked this path. He knew betrayal, grief, and suffering beyond what we can imagine, yet He continued to love. He trusted His Father's plan, even in the darkest hours. And He served until His last breath.

Your pain does not disqualify you from purpose; it may actually deepen it. The scars you carry can become the very places where God's light shines brightest, offering hope to others who walk the same road.

Jason Kesack, Law Enforcement Officer

14. Posttraumatic growth isn't a destination; it's a way of living differently, intentionally.

The journey of growth I have experienced is not perfect. There have been ups and downs, leaps forward and slides backward. The key is to keep moving forward with a positive purpose and to avoid destructive isolation.

Where I once dwelled on things, overthinking and obsessing, I now try to talk them through with other healthy members of the warrior community. This allows me to grow rather than destroy. Growth is something I must practice daily, keeping it at the forefront of my purpose.

I remind myself that my mind must be kept in shape to handle life in a positive way, and that comes through positive practices and surrounding myself with positive people.

Dr. Benjamin Iobst, US Army Combat Veteran (Iraq War) and Law Enforcement Officer

15. PTG isn't about denial; it's about integration, discovery, and strength.

My journey with Posttraumatic growth began when I finally gave myself the space to validate my own traumatic experiences. Surviving the unimaginable did not mean I had to forget, minimize, or compare my pain. It meant I had to face it. Real growth does not come from denial. It comes from integrating what happened into who we are now. True growth is about acknowledging our pain, honoring how it shaped us, and taking responsibility for how we carry it forward. It is about offering ourselves grace, love, compassion, and patience through each stage of healing, because recovery is never linear.

When I denied my trauma, I remained stuck in cycles of shame and blame, trapped by negative thoughts, behaviors, and emotions. Choosing growth allowed me to step beyond what hurt me. It gave me the ability to see my story through a new lens, helping me rebuild, reimagine, and reinvent myself.

What once was only a source of pain has become a catalyst for something brighter. My trauma taught me resilience, connection, and strength. It revealed who I truly am. The path to growth is not easy, but it shows us what we are capable of enduring and creating. What we learn along the way becomes the foundation for everything we build next.

Jennifer Aleman, US Army Combat Veteran (War on Terror)

16. A deeper sense of purpose often starts with surviving the unimaginable.

Life is challenging, but until we face the ultimate challenge of surviving a deadly event, we can fail to see the purpose in it. When we sense the potential for our own loss of life and live through it, we find an understanding that many cannot relate to. Those who share that experience develop a bond that can be difficult to explain, or even considered a disconnection from the rest of the world.

The connection between shared suffering or danger establishes an unspoken wisdom only found in that moment between those who shared it. Often, friends and family of soldiers and First Responders feel a disconnection where there once was none. It is this shared experience that reshapes them and those who lived it. The burdened may find it unexplainable to their loved ones, leading to resentment or misunderstanding. This can manifest as an unwillingness to share, despite the fact that only those who were there can truly understand.

Reconnection without suppression with family, friends, and society is difficult without the peers who experienced the challenge with you. Soldiers and First Responders must go through the process of accepting their experience and understanding their new knowledge of life. They can then apply that experience to their lives without suppressing the fears and emotions they felt. This can lead to purposeful integration into the social network of family, friends, and the greater community.

Robert Smith, US Army Combat Veteran (Desert Storm and Iraq War)

17. The pain that almost broke you may one day become the reason you help others heal.

During my time in the Marine Corps, I was almost always angry. That anger led me to argue with senior enlisted, treat the local population poorly, and treat myself as if I did not deserve to feel anything other than rage. When I came home in 2010, the anger was no longer needed, but it was still very much alive. My Platoon Sergeant once told me, "What made you good down range will make you the worst civilian when you get out. It is up to you to figure out what you need to leave here."

For eight years, I held on to that anger, and it dragged me into some dark places. After finding recovery in 2016, I finally reached the point where I no longer wanted to live that way. I told myself, I may not know how, but I am going to figure this out.

With the support of like-minded people who had made progress of their own, the anger began to melt away. It was replaced with care and concern for myself and, more importantly, for others. I learned that anger can be transformed into passion and that my shortcomings were really strengths taken to an unhealthy extreme. Bringing those qualities back into balance is one of the most valuable skills I have learned.

I believe everything I have experienced has prepared me so that someone else does not have to go through it alone.

Justin Wright, USMC Combat Veteran (Iraq War)

18. What if this scar is where your calling begins?

On November 11, Veterans Day, I left home for the first time, boarding a plane to Lackland Air Force Base in Texas for Basic Training. Immediately upon arrival, I was herded into a small square and greeted with shouted orders from every direction, a true TI welcome. I adapted quickly, excelling in fitness tests and classes, with only minor uniform infractions.

Warrior Week was the ultimate test: field training, M16 qualification, and the unforgettable gas chamber. The final challenge was a grueling mile and a half obstacle course, which I finished among the first. Proud of my achievement, I made the mistake of celebrating with cake in the chow hall. Three TIs descended, firing questions I could not answer under pressure. Humiliated, I was ordered to see my First Sergeant, "MSGT Big Momma Pain," who washed me back a week.

Alone in the barracks, negative thoughts flooded in, but I resolved not to quit. My new TI, a former Marine, was the toughest on base. The second time through Warrior Week, I pushed harder and graduated, though my mother, who had arrived early, missed the ceremony.

On graduation day, my TI told me, "Airman Carson, congratulations, you are born again hard."

That experience taught me that setbacks are opportunities. I was washed back because I froze under pressure, but it shaped my resilience. Since then, I have advised military leadership, spoken on podcasts, and delivered keynote speeches. What was once a source of shame has become a story that has inspired thousands.

Thomas J. Carson, US Air Force Veteran

19. Trauma disrupts identity; growth reclaims it with clarity.

My first experience with trauma was growing up in a household filled with yelling, physical abuse, substance abuse, and alcohol. It was common to see my mother with black and blue eyes from my father's violence. At just seven or eight years old, I often stepped between them, trying to protect her, something no child should ever have to do. My father seldom struck me, but there were a few times when he did, including once when he held me underwater in our backyard pool until I nearly lost consciousness. My grandmother intervened just in time to save my life.

These experiences scarred me deeply as a child. As I grew older, I turned to alcohol and drugs to numb the pain and memories. I carried a lot of anger but found healthier outlets through sports such as wrestling, football, and martial arts. Physical activity became an outlet for my stress and a way to calm the nightmares.

Eventually, I joined the Navy and was stationed on an aircraft carrier, working on the flight deck. I came to appreciate what I call organized and controlled chaos, which gave me a sense of order and purpose.

Later in life, I was fortunate to join our Tribe, where I found qualified friends and mentors who guided me and helped me stop abusing alcohol. They were instrumental in restoring my sense of worth and helping me become a productive and positive citizen. I owe my life to this group and will never forget what they have done for me.

Kenny Seagraves, US Navy Veteran

20. After chaos, many discover they are more connected to life than before.

Looking back at my struggles with PTSD, I was fortunate to be invited to a group meeting with others who also live with its challenges. This is not something faced only by military Veterans. First Responders, emergency technicians, police officers, and firefighters also suffer. It affects not only men, but women as well. The group provides comfort, compassion, and understanding to everyone who attends, all without ridicule or prejudice. It is a place where you can share both struggles and accomplishments.

In these meetings, you hear about many difficulties, including PTSD, depression, anxiety, anger, substance abuse, and trust issues. It is striking to realize how many people carry similar burdens. Many struggles begin at a young age, and people do their best to cope with them as life moves forward.

Fortunately, groups like this exist and are open to anyone in need. They are a powerful support system. Sometimes all it takes is a phone call, a conversation with a friend, or searching the mental health network to find help.

You must allow yourself to grow. You owe it to yourself to see where life can take you. And you do not need to do it alone. Doctors, counselors, advocates, and clergy can guide you. Remember, you are in the driver's seat of your life. Take the path that helps you become the best version of yourself.

Chuck Durback, US Army Combat Veteran (Vietnam War)

21. The world may seem smaller after trauma, but your inner world can grow deeper.

We all experience the outer world in our own kind of virtual reality. We perceive the world through our senses, and then the mind creates a narrative. When we see, what we are really experiencing is light reflecting off an object and interacting with the cornea and retina in our eyes. This light is converted into electrical signals that travel through the nervous system to the brain's visual center, where images are recreated. Our other senses function in similar ways, forming our personal depiction of the outer world.

It is our inner self that perceives the outside world. This is where thoughts occur, emotions arise, preferences take shape, and where delusions and doubt can live. Recovery from traumatic experiences often awakens a new awareness of this inner world that was not available before.

My trauma came from prolonged exposure to combat. Recovery has been a process that continues nearly 20 years later. With help along the way, I discovered that within myself exists a place that is always undisturbed and at peace, no matter what is happening around me or within my mind. This peaceful awareness is our natural state of being, present in all of us.

The distractions of the modern world are endless if we give them our attention. It takes a steady commitment to be still and calm the mind, but from this stillness we recognize our peaceful awareness as the true baseline of life. As Thich Nhat Hanh taught, "the way out is in."

Jeremy Gann, US Army Combat Veteran (Iraq and Afghanistan Wars)

22. When you endure what you thought you couldn't, you redefine what you're capable of.

When I left the military in November 2011, I was going through some hard times. I had just ended a toxic relationship, I had no money, and I had lost my sense of purpose. I was one step away from being homeless. I was given the opportunity to live in my mother's basement, and after months of self-pity and sorrow, I decided to go back to school using my GI Bill.

The first few semesters were very challenging. I was close to thirty years old when I started, and my background was in vocational training, not traditional academics. I lacked the math, English, and science foundation that many younger students already had. I remember going before and after class to seek extra help from my professors. With persistence, I passed all my courses and earned a degree from Northampton Community College.

After graduating, I went on to obtain a degree from Penn State University, and today I am working toward my master's degree in executive leadership. Each challenge we overcome redefines what we are capable of.

Scripture reminds us in Jeremiah 29:11, "For I know the plans I have for you," declares the Lord, "plans to prosper you and not to harm you, plans to give you hope and a future." The Lord places no limits on what we can achieve. Every challenge He puts before us is shaping us into who He intends us to become.

Thomas J. Carson, US Air Force Veteran

23. PTG is often found in stillness, silence, and shared stories.

Through my journey, I have engaged in many different modalities of treatment for PTSD and a TBI, stemming from my military and police career. Through the program established by Restored Warrior and Struggle Well, we come together in a closed group of like-minded individuals who have walked similar paths. While the specific events that caused our PTSD may differ, most of us identify with the same struggles and trauma responses.

Participating in Posttraumatic growth and sharing our experiences from the readings helps us connect with one another. It allows us to heal as a group rather than as isolated individuals, knowing we are not alone and that our voices are heard. By sharing openly, we prevent those thoughts from continuing to rent space in our minds.

In this group, individuals support one another by sharing what has worked for them. If someone has faced a similar situation and found effective solutions, they offer insight into what helped. I have learned that instead of letting rage consume me or simply fighting to be okay, I can channel that energy into something positive. When anger builds, I take it to the gym, work it out, and put it away until needed again. Trauma does not have to destroy us. Growth allows us to transform it into strength.

The camaraderie we share here is what many of us lost, or only thought we had, in our First Responder careers. In this group, those bonds are genuine. We operate with one mission, one understanding, and one connection. No matter when or where, someone will be there.

David Alercia, USMC Veteran, Retired Law Enforcement Officer

24. The best parts of you may have been shaped in the worst of times.

The best parts of me emerged during the darkest of times. My battle with drugs and alcohol nearly destroyed everything: my health, my mind, my family, my job, and my will to live. I have been through hell and back, staring down the bottle, convinced it was my only companion, only to realize it was the very thing trying to bury me.

Those nights that seemed destined to break me were the same ones that forged me. Every blackout, every withdrawal, every time I swore I was done and then fell again, they carved something in me I could not see at the time: grit, humility, resilience, and the kind of strength that only comes from crawling out of your own grave and refusing to go back in.

Here is the truth: drugs and alcohol were not the problem. It was the chaos, fear, sadness, hurt, and resentment I carried. My failure to face them properly created anxiety, depression, and explosive anger. Ultimately, it led to isolation and a mind that spiraled deeper into the storm.

I will not sugarcoat it. This fight is ugly and real. If you are in the thick of it, know this: your worst days do not define you; they are shaping you. Every scar and every stumble is proof that you are still swinging. And the best version of you is still there, waiting on the other side of the fight.

"Out of the hottest fire comes the strongest steel." – Chinese Proverb

Nate Laskey, USMC Combat Veteran (Iraq War)

25. The road to growth is uncomfortable, but so is staying stuck.

For Veterans and First Responders, change often comes through fire. We know the sting of discomfort-not only in training or dangerous calls, but in the quiet aftermath. Growth asks us to face memories we would rather lock away, emotions we would rather numb, and truths about ourselves that are hard to swallow. But staying stuck is uncomfortable too. It means sleepless nights that never change, a short fuse that keeps burning bridges, and the sense that life is happening around you, not through you. While growth can be exhausting, it is the kind of discomfort that leads somewhere better.

Consider Louis Zamperini, an Olympic runner turned World War II bombardier. After his plane crashed in the Pacific, he survived 47 days adrift at sea, only to be captured and brutally mistreated as a prisoner of war. Returning home, he battled rage, nightmares, and alcoholism, trapped in a cycle of pain. Only when he embraced forgiveness through his faith did he find true freedom.

The road was not easy, but it led to restoration, purpose, and hope. Growth means choosing the hard steps today so tomorrow is lighter. That might mean starting therapy, opening up in a support group, forgiving yourself, or letting someone else help carry the load.

God promises we are "being renewed day by day" (2 Corinthians 4:16). Renewal is active. It demands courage and calls us forward. Each small step is choosing life over stagnation.

You are worth the journey.

Jason Kesack, Law Enforcement Officer

26. People who experience PTG often discover their values with newfound urgency.

Anything can be used as motivation when I am open to a new perspective. I am not my past or the lies that negative thinking tells me. Growth that comes through discomfort can be an asset, something to harness and use for strength.

Justin Wright, USMC Combat Veteran (Iraq War)

27. Posttraumatic growth is about turning wounds into wisdom.

My journey with PTSD began in 1966 when I joined the US Army. After training at Fort Gordon and Fort Eustis, I married in June 1967, welcomed a child in October, and deployed to Vietnam that December. I was stationed at An Khe, home of the 1st Cavalry Division, and later moved to LZ Sharon near Quang Tri.

During the Tet Offensive of 1968, I faced my first traumatic combat experience. Soldiers are expected to be tough and fearless, but I was scared and unsure of what would happen. I knew I had to protect the base and my fellow soldiers. That first moment of decision, was it them or me, has stayed with me ever since. The military is excellent at training for war but does not teach you how to return to society. That part you must figure out on your own.

When I came home, I worked for 16 years but never spoke of Vietnam. Few even knew I had served. I struggled with anxiety, depression, anger, nightmares, drinking, and isolation. At the time, I did not know what PTSD was or that help was available.

It took more than 40 years before I admitted I needed help. In 2009, a fellow Veteran convinced me to attend a VA meeting in Allentown, and that was the beginning of my recovery.

In 2024, I joined a group of Veterans and First Responders who share openly and without judgment. My final thought is simple: it is never too late to seek help.

Chuck Durback, US Army Combat Veteran (Vietnam War)

28. Real courage is facing the aftermath, and still choosing meaning.

As First Responders, trauma and adverse experiences are part of the job. I began in emergency services at 16 and had no idea how to process what I saw. The best I could do was watch how others reacted and try to copy their behavior. It would take nearly 10 years and countless traumatic events before I began to process them in a meaningful way.

As I matured in my career, I learned to take smaller pieces of trauma and talk them through with like-minded responders. Sharing what I saw, how I felt, and how I reacted helped me work through the experience without repressing my emotions or turning to destructive behaviors such as alcohol or tobacco. Still, there were times when the weight of stress and trauma built up, and I lashed out at coworkers or those around me. I was unpleasant and short-tempered, more defensive than productive.

Over time, I learned the value of stepping away from work, decompressing, and investing in hobbies and family. This allowed me to handle hard calls and difficult patients without letting them linger in the same way.

Today, trauma and stress are no longer hidden in emergency response. They are openly acknowledged as part of the profession. Trauma is not a surprise side effect anymore-it is something I recognize, accept, and manage with awareness.

William Carver, Paramedic, Former Firefighter

29. When you reflect instead of retreat, you make room for growth.

Before I began my journey of growth, I spent years refusing to acknowledge my emotions or the effects that my experiences were having on my mental, physical, and social health. I played endless mind games with myself, denying that anything was wrong. I would do mental backflips to avoid dealing with the truth, often numbing myself with alcohol in the process.

When I finally began to do the work, by accepting the help of others and keeping my body and mind clean, it was uncomfortable at first. It felt like cleaning out old infected wounds. Yet it was also a relief, because deep down I knew I had not been handling things well. That process opened the door to a new way of living I did not realize was possible. Where I once saw only limitations, pain, and unhealthy coping, I now found opportunities to grow and thrive.

This was only the beginning of the journey, but life has since become something I enjoy rather than endure. Difficult moments still come, but I now approach them differently. Instead of constantly managing damage, I can make responsible decisions that strengthen my life and the lives of those around me.

Growth is not about ignoring pain but about facing it honestly, healing from it, and learning to live fully again.

Dr. Benjamin Iobst, US Army Combat Veteran (Iraq War) and Retired Law Enforcement Officer

30. It's not about "getting over it." It's about getting through it, and growing because of it.

I can remember asking, "Why is this happening to me?" and "When can I move on?" as I went through the most difficult time in my life. I was so focused on making physical progress that I almost overlooked the mental and emotional strides I was making. It is often said that we learn more from our losses than from our wins. In the same way, trauma, while it never feels like it in the moment, can provide opportunities for growth and expansion as we move forward.

There are some things we can never truly get over: the loss of a loved one, a debilitating injury or illness, the loss of a career, or other life altering events that become a permanent part of our story. We can, however, get through them. As we move forward, we can carry the positive aspects, the lessons learned, the love felt, the good times shared, while choosing to leave the pain behind.

The list of possible traumas is almost endless. At times it can feel like a giant wheel on a game show spinning until it lands on the trauma you "win." Like many of you, I did not get to choose my trauma, and I doubt this is the one I would have chosen. What we do get to choose, often the only choice we have, is what we carry forward from it.

Matthew Rush, Retired Law Enforcement Officer

31. You can hold both the weight of the trauma and the light of the transformation.

Life has a way of teaching us that two seemingly opposing truths can exist at once. To hold the weight of trauma is to acknowledge the pain, the loss, and the scars that shape us. It is the quiet admission that what happened matters, that it has altered the way we see the world, and perhaps even the way we see ourselves. Carrying that weight is not weakness; it is proof that our hearts have been tender enough to feel deeply, even when that depth came with ache.

And yet, alongside that heaviness, there is the light of transformation, a glow that does not erase the pain but illuminates the path forward. Transformation does not mean forgetting; it means allowing the pain to become the soil in which new strength, compassion, and wisdom can grow. This light may flicker at first, but over time it expands, showing us that we are not only what has happened to us, but also who we choose to become because of it.

To hold both is to live in wholeness, not forcing ourselves to be only healed or only hurt, but allowing both realities to coexist. It is in this delicate balance that we discover resilience: the quiet courage to carry the shadows while walking toward the dawn. The weight keeps us grounded; the light keeps us moving. Together, they make us more human, more open, and more alive.

Kate Murray, Law Enforcement Officer

32. Through Posttraumatic growth, I've come to see that life did not happen to me, but for me.

I never really understood trauma or the impact it had on my brain. Back then, I just thought these were the cards I was dealt, and I did what I had to do to survive. As a kid, I wondered why these things were happening to me and what I had done to deserve it. Living in fear of my dad's authority, I struggled with my identity and spent years searching for my place in the world.

The military gave me structure and purpose, but when I came back to civilian life, I started to realize how much those earlier wounds shaped my outlook. I grew up in the inner city, saw a lot of violence, and lost people close to me. I never processed those deaths; I just numbed the pain with alcohol and substances. That left me angry, resentful, and feeling alone.

Posttraumatic growth opened a new door. I learned I was stronger than I realized, strong enough to keep getting up after every fall. I met others, in groups and workshops, who carried similar struggles. I realized I wasn't alone, and together we built tools to turn pain into growth.

I can't change what happened, but I can choose how it shapes my healing. Today, I'm not a victim. I'm a man creating his own destiny.

Kevin McCloud, US Army Veteran

33. With healing, even the worst chapters can become powerful prologues.

The most challenging experiences of my life, both from the Iraq War and my time as a police officer, can be used in two very different ways. The first is as an excuse to destroy myself, to blame the world for all its pain, and to isolate. The second is to use these experiences as fuel for growth, to take them and put them to good work, to turn them into the foundation of a purpose-driven existence.

The choice of what to do with them is mine, and I have the power to choose.

> *Dr. Benjamin Iobst, US Army Combat Veteran (Iraq War) and Law Enforcement Officer*

34. Some of the strongest roots grow after the storm.

Having recently retired from city policing after 22 years, I reflect upon my career and the impact it has had on me as a person. I think of how I was able to navigate a difficult job where trauma and traumatic experiences were a reality.

Luck certainly played a part, but more important was my root system, to continue the tree analogy. When I started my career, I was an untested rookie who felt I could take on the world. In truth, my roots were as fragile as a sapling. Over time, as I gained experience, I learned not only from my successes but, more importantly, from my failures. Each experience added strength to my roots. As I progressed in my career, I felt stronger and more firmly grounded.

It was not until I encountered trauma, and dealt with the aftermath of those events, that I realized a different type of inner strength. Surviving the traumatic moments was one thing; coping with the Posttraumatic effects was another. Trauma and its aftermath are not predetermined successes or failures. What made the difference was my attitude and mindset, my choice to turn trauma into something positive. My roots grew deeper and stronger because of those experiences. I now know that I can not only persevere but also thrive.

John Turoczi, Retired Law Enforcement Officer

35. Growth after trauma often means you stop trying to be who you were and start becoming who you are.

During my career, I watched other officers engage in destructive behaviors and thought, "How could they?" Over time I learned that self destruction does not always look like cutting, drug use, or suicide. It can be anything that damages what we value most. I eventually realized I was burying my own stress in behaviors that were quietly destroying my world. By 2008, I was living in a rented house with a ruined knee, a family that had distanced itself, and nights where I wondered, "Why am I bothering? Who would miss me?"

After every low point, I eventually got angry enough to fight back. I reached a moment where I was done with self-destruction. Instead of letting others dictate my story, I chose to take it back. I began showing up as my true self at work, reengaging with my family, and investing in life again. The more I lived as the person I always believed myself to be, the more things began to change. I stopped apologizing for every decision and started owning the choices that shaped me.

After my first divorce, I wrestled with feelings of failure. Yet what I once saw as fatal flaws became insights I could use to help others. By recognizing my own destructive patterns, I could guide those on the same dangerous path. In reaching out, I found my own healing-not as penance, but as a choice to grow.

John Hill, USMC Combat Veteran (Desert Storm), Retired Law Enforcement Officer

36. Growth comes when one reflects honestly on life and lets both pain and blessings shape who they become.

When I reflect on my life story to this point (age 60), I see how both good and difficult experiences have shaped who I am. Central to that journey has been my moral compass, established through Christianity. Two people were especially influential in guiding me: my mother and our minister in the church where I grew up. I accepted Jesus Christ as my Lord and Savior early in life, and ever since, my faith has provided direction and strength.

My professional path has been challenging but deeply rewarding. Because of the Lord, I have had perseverance and endurance through trials. I have worked in community mental health, forensic juvenile probation, and later served as Director of Forensic Services. For the past 26 years, I have also been privileged to serve as a therapist in private practice. Over these decades, I have walked alongside tens of thousands of people facing hardships, including some of the most painful circumstances imaginable.

Through it all, I have practiced what I call soul stewardship. This begins with awareness of my relationship with myself, guided by my moral compass. It requires seeing reality as clearly as possible, then choosing to do what is right and healthy according to that guidance. Practicing soul stewardship has consistently given me clarity and growth, even in the most difficult seasons of life.

Drew Taylor, Probation Officer

37. The journey doesn't erase the pain-it transforms your relationship to it.

Medically retiring after five knee surgeries in the middle of my military career taught me how many forms pain can take. I was prepared to live with chronic physical pain, something many who have served before and after me have come to accept. But nothing prepared me for the invisible wounds: the deep emotional pain of losing my abled body, my career, and the identity I had built around both, all before the age of 27. That kind of loss left me isolated, grieving, and untethered. The combination of physical injury and despair only worsened my health, trapping me in a cycle of decline.

Instead of continuing that cycle, I began to break it. I stopped feeding the patterns of pain and started creating new ones, where even the smallest moments of joy became a priority. I worked to shift my view of pain from something purely negative to something meaningful, a signal from within reminding me when I needed rest, care, or reflection.

Now, after 22 surgeries and a diagnosis of Complex Regional Pain Syndrome, one of the highest rated conditions on the McGill Pain Scale, I see that my pain has not disappeared but my relationship with it has changed. Walking the path of Posttraumatic growth taught me something vital: you cannot heal the body without also healing the mind.

My pain is no longer a punishment. It is a testament to my strength, my resilience, and the storms I have survived.

Jennifer Aleman, US Army Combat Veteran (War on Terror)

38. Meaning can rise even from rubble.

There is something that is often overlooked in times of struggle and trauma, usually for good reason, as they can be all-consuming. That is the fact that our struggles provide us with the opportunity to discover a new path. It is sometimes after our darkest moments that we realize what we truly have inside of us and where we can best direct those talents. I know that this was true for me.

When I was at my lowest point, I had no idea that my struggle would provide me with not only a new awareness of the strength inside of me, but also a new direction for my life. I was grappling with what would be next for me since my career path was forever altered. I was never going to be able to physically do what I had loved doing. I was having a hard time imagining my life differently, and it was then that I received a card from my sister which contained a single line attributed to Lao Tzu: "When I let go of who I am, I become who I might be."

This marked a point of change for me. I used the pain and darkness I had experienced to redirect my life into efforts to be of assistance to others going through their difficult times. In helping others during their rough times, I not only shared what I had learned on my journey, but I also learned from them.

For the first time in my life, I feel like I am doing what I was meant to do, and none of it would have happened if I had not been knocked off my old path. It may be a different calling for you, but if you look for them, there are opportunities that never would have been available if you had not gone through your trauma.

Matthew Rush, Retired Law Enforcement Officer

39. After trauma, priorities often sharpen, and trivial things fall away.

Being downrange in Iraq was an experience like none other I have had to this day. You experience trauma as it comes and stow it away for the time being. When I came back home, much of this unpacked into my life without me even being aware of it.

I will tell you this, though I suffered, I found meaning in it. After processing, and continuing to process my trauma, I have discovered new meaning in life. Instead of the Lt. Dan syndrome I once carried, I have turned it into appreciation for life. I am alive, and others are not. I have the responsibility to live the life they cannot.

I have turned the pain into motivation: going back to school, working on myself to become the best version of me, and being of service to others who are also on this journey.

Justin Wright, USMC Combat Veteran (Iraq War)

40. In the space left by trauma, some find new creativity, compassion, and connection.

In the space left by trauma, I discovered both darkness and unexpected light. Leaving the Army was harder than I ever imagined, not because I missed the uniform, but because I missed the sense of purpose, the brotherhood, and the structure that gave every day meaning. When I came home, PTSD was not just nightmares; it was silence, anger, and the feeling that I no longer belonged anywhere.

But in that empty space, something began to shift. At first, it was only survival, writing down my thoughts, picking up small creative projects, and forcing myself to connect with people I trusted. Over time, those practices became lifelines. The same discipline that carried me through deployment began to guide me through healing. I learned that vulnerability was not weakness but another form of courage.

Today, the scars remain, but they are part of my story rather than the end of it. Through compassion, creativity, and connection with other Veterans and First Responders, I have found a new mission: to heal, to grow, and to help others know they are not alone. Trauma took much from me, but it also left space to rebuild, a space I now fill with purpose and hope.

Freddie Reed, US Army Combat Veteran (Iraq War)

41. What if your recovery is part of someone else's survival?

Deployment for me was not just about leading a small signal team on a mission; it was about leaving behind my two young children during a painful divorce. While setting up critical communications under wartime orders, I was also carrying the invisible weight of single motherhood. I returned home with heightened anxiety, nightmares, and a nervous system stuck in survival mode. Yet I was expected to instantly become the nurturing mother my children needed.

The military trained me to lead, make split second decisions, and suppress emotion. These traits were praised in uniform but stood in painful contrast to the tenderness required in parenting. PTSD was often discussed in terms of addiction or recklessness, but rarely in terms of how trauma reshapes a mother. I found myself reactive, overwhelmed, and despising the version of myself trauma had created.

In time, I realized healing was not only something I owed myself, it was vital to my children's survival. I had to unlearn suppression and relearn how to regulate, connect, and nurture with intention. My recovery became the foundation for their growth and sense of safety.

They saw my pain, but more importantly, they saw my progress. Now, as my youngest prepares for college, I see how our shared resilience shaped who they are. My recovery was not just my journey, it was the key to theirs. My healing became their survival.

Jennifer Aleman, US Army Combat Veteran (War On Terror)

42. Growth doesn't erase grief; it walks beside it.

During the Iraq War, several of my friends I was serving with were killed. When I first returned home, I carried their memories like a ball and chain, wondering why I lived and they did not. That thought process took me to some very dark places.

Through working with other Veterans and First Responders, changing my perspective with therapy and wellness practices, and embracing healing, I am now living a life full of possibilities. Where I once carried their memories as wounds and survivor's guilt, I now carry them as a reason to live a good life.

I live with purpose where they no longer can, and I bring their memory with me into places that honor them and are filled with hope and possibility.

> *Dr. Benjamin Iobst, US Army Combat Veteran (Iraq War) and Law Enforcement Officer*

43. PTG is often sparked by connection and healing in community, not isolation.

In March of 2004, I deployed to Iraq and served with the First Cavalry Division outside of Baghdad. When I returned home in 2005, I thought I was fine and did not need to address the trauma that began in my early childhood and followed me into adulthood. I chose to isolate and avoid rather than face those demons. After serious complications from surgery in 2021, my issues progressed until I fell into the darkest time of my life. I feared losing my family, my career, and even my life.

I soon realized I could not manage alone and needed to reach out for help. I began therapy, learned meditation, and leaned on my family support system more than ever. I was also given the opportunity to attend a weekly support group for Veterans and First Responders. In that group, I discovered I was not alone in my past trauma. Others had lived through similar experiences, and the shared connections created a safe place for honest disclosure.

That community gave me a sense of belonging and brotherhood that I had been missing. It sparked my journey toward Posttraumatic growth and showed me the strength that comes from connection. I now have a tribe of brothers I can turn to in times of need and who I can support when they need uplifting. The truth I have found is simple: the tribe is always stronger than any one person.

Shane Schmeckenbecher, US Army Combat Veteran (Iraq War), Probation Officer

44. After trauma, your presence becomes a quiet rebellion against despair.

A samurai proverb says, "Fall seven times and stand up eight." I hold this close to my heart because I have fallen more times than I can count. Trauma, grief, and hardship have left me on the ground wondering if I could get back up. Each time I rise, I discover a strength in myself I did not know was there.

Standing up again does not mean the pain disappears. It means I refuse to let the pain be the end of my story. Every scar I carry is proof that I got back up. I remind myself that I am not defined by how many times I have been knocked down, but by the choice to rise again.

For me, Posttraumatic growth is about choosing to rise, to live, and to prove to myself that I am not broken.

Dr. Benjamin Iobst, US Army Combat Veteran (Iraq War) and Law Enforcement Officer

45. From crisis can come clarity.

For years, my identity was rooted in being a police officer. I took pride in serving, but the trauma from both my adolescence and my time in uniform left deep scars. PTSD and alcoholism eventually consumed me, forcing me to resign from the career that had once defined my purpose. Without the badge, I felt stripped of who I was. Suicidal thoughts and attempts became part of my daily struggle.

What followed, however, was an unexpected process of transformation. Through therapy, faith, community support, and connection with others who had walked similar paths, I began to experience Posttraumatic growth. Rather than being crushed by trauma, I learned to rebuild myself through it. Healing required vulnerability, humility, honesty, and the courage to seek help. In that process, I discovered that my experiences, while painful, did not make me less. They gave me depth, empathy, and resilience.

Posttraumatic growth did not erase the hardships I faced, but it allowed me to find meaning within them. My journey through PTSD and addiction gave me a renewed sense of purpose. Sobriety restored clarity, and connection restored hope. Today, I use my story not only to continue my own healing but also to encourage others who are struggling.

I may no longer wear the uniform, but I have found an identity far greater: a man who has endured, grown, and now seeks to serve by showing that healing is possible.

Brian Sabo, Former Police Officer

46. The most profound wisdom often follows struggle.

Operation Wayne Grey, Task Force Swift in the Plei Trap Valley RVN, 1 March to April 14, 1969. Little is known or written about this Op, but it remains with me daily. I was a squad leader with Bravo 3/12, 4th Infantry Division. We pursued the 66th NVA Regiment throughout the Central Highlands of Vietnam, from the Cambodian border and back. On 11 and 12 March, we encountered heavy contact. We lost many good men in those two days. I was wounded and medevac'd on the 12th, spent months in hospitals, and was discharged in 1970.

As a civilian, I had no direction. I suffered with PTS, anxiety, depression, and anger. The slightest noise or action would trigger me, but like many of my generation, we were too strong and too proud to seek help. I pushed forward, using alcohol to deal with the memories and pain. I married and we had three sons. My father was an alcoholic and not much of a role model. I tried to be a good father but failed many times. Living with me was a challenge for my wife and children.

In 2018, I met a former member of my unit. After months, he convinced me to seek help. I was treated by the VA and began reconnecting with other Veterans. It wasn't until I joined a group of Veterans and First Responders that my life truly moved in a positive direction. Sharing our stories and trauma has helped me see life differently. I still have issues, but weekly meetings and the bonds we've built keep me moving forward. I am now struggling better.

My goal is to Struggle Well.

John Kukitz, US Army Combat Veteran (Vietnam War)

47. Healing is not going back to who you were; it's becoming someone wiser.

After leaving the military, I thought the chaos I carried inside would never quiet down. The weight of PTSD felt like it cut me off from the world, from people, and even from myself. Yet slowly, through the pain, I began to see a different path, one built not on shutting down but on reconnecting with life.

Becoming a Reiki Master was a turning point. At first, it was simply a way to find calm and let my nervous system rest. Over time, it became a doorway to healing. The energy work helped me move beyond survival and toward balance, and it showed me that connection does not end when the uniform comes off; it just transforms.

I began to give back, guiding other Veterans and First Responders who also carry invisible wounds. In serving them, I found my own strength growing. I realized that healing is not just personal, it is shared. Every time I held space for someone else's story, I felt a little more whole myself.

The chaos that once defined me no longer has the final word. In its place is compassion, community, and a renewed sense of purpose. My journey is proof that after trauma, life can become more connected, not less, and that giving back can be the most powerful way of healing forward.

Freddie Reed, US Army Combat Veteran (Iraq War)

48. You didn't choose the trauma, but you can choose the transformation.

Trauma is what we experience, whether from many exposures over time or from a single event. If we do not work on our mental health, those experiences continue to shape us and prevent us from achieving Posttraumatic growth. Whatever the cause, trauma creates a blueprint in the brain, leaving symptoms and behaviors that ripple through every part of life.

I enlisted in the US Army in April 1974 and was assigned to the Military Police Corps. The Vietnam War was officially declared over, and front-line troops were returning home, but smaller forces still remained until the fall of Saigon in April 1975. The military was shifting into a Cold War role, providing peacekeeping and security for thousands of Vietnamese refugees.

That transition prepared me for a 22-year career in law enforcement from 1977 to 1999. Over that time, I served in patrol, criminal investigations, undercover work in the Vice and Intelligence Division, and as a Detective Sergeant in the Central Investigation Division. I endured 16 injuries, one line-of-duty shooting, and a serious motor vehicle accident that kept me out most of 1996. My trauma exposures were many, but no resources were available to help us cope in healthy ways.

It was not until my third marriage was failing and I admitted I had a drug and alcohol problem that I realized I needed to change. Choosing to advocate for myself, seek help, and learn new coping skills not only saved my life but made me a better person in every area of it.

Dr. Thomas Ritter, US Army Veteran, Retired Law Enforcement Officer

49. Posttraumatic growth means finding strength, wisdom, and purpose in the struggles that once nearly broke you.

"There is nothing like the heart of a volunteer." I am not sure where I first heard that saying, but I live by it. I don't hesitate to help; whether it's at an accident, looking for lost animals, or even rescuing an alligator, I'm there.

Becoming an EMT, paramedic, firefighter, and now a police sergeant felt like a natural progression for me. I've always wanted to serve, and I've lived it all.

One of the hardest experiences I ever faced came during a rather aggressive police call when I sustained a cardiac arrest. It was traumatic in every way. I fought hard to come back from the physical damage, but the mental trauma lasted much longer. I never expected how difficult that recovery would be.

Joining the Tribe has helped me more than I could have imagined. It has given me a place to share my thoughts with others who have also been in dark places. The truth is, you can't talk to most people about feelings of loss, fear, and survival in the same way. But in this group, there is understanding. That shared connection makes healing possible.

What I did was who I was. My accident forced me to stop and think deeply about where I go from here. Through reflection and support, I've grown mentally and emotionally. Posttraumatic growth means finding purpose and realizing the love of my wife, my family, and my dogs-the greatest gift of my journey.

Christopher Hendricks, Law Enforcement Officer and Paramedic

50. The weight of what you've endured can strengthen the foundation of who you become.

My greatest trauma shrank my external world considerably. Physically, I could not move the way I once did, and being a police officer, along with many of my off-duty pursuits, was no longer an option. These realities took their inevitable toll on my mental health. It was then that I realized the only things I could still control were how I thought about and reacted to these events.

I turned to meditation and began studying Stoic and other philosophies. This channeled my energy away from my physical self into my mind and spirit. I discovered that the mind is far stronger than the body, and I grew as I learned about myself in ways I never had before. I built a new understanding of who I was and what I was capable of. Even if I could change the past, I would not trade my experiences of pain and trauma for anything.

I have become a better father, friend, husband, and person than I was before. There is no doubt that my trauma permanently changed me physically. Mentally, I also came out of it a different person than I had been going in. And the truth is, that is a good thing.

Matthew Rush, Retired Law Enforcement Officer

51. Let your healing be proof that something beautiful can come from what was broken.

We have all felt the depths of being broken. But broken does not mean beyond repair. Just like setting a broken bone, healing requires a process. It comes with pain, frustration, and eventually new growth. When we commit to that process and do the work to find ourselves again, we are reintroduced to someone we never knew before, someone with strength, courage, and perseverance.

We are always growing and learning. In healing, we also give others the opportunity to witness what is possible through the changes happening within us, and that is a true gift.

Give yourself the gift of turning your brokenness into beauty. The road will not be easy, and the stumbles along the way will test what we are truly made of. But the clearing at the end, the renewal, the strength, the light, is what many would call a miracle.

Amy J. Iobst, EMT

52. You're not just surviving, you're evolving.

Traumatic experiences and cumulative trauma are, by any definition, incredibly difficult and stressful to endure. Experiences of this magnitude are always life-altering and often life-changing. But altering in what way, positively or negatively? The answer is entirely up to the person affected.

There are really two options. One option is to let the experience beat you, to wallow in prolonged self-pity and become comfortable in the role of victim. To numb the problem with drugs or alcohol. The inevitable result is a diminished quality of life.

The second option is to face the trauma in a positive and realistic way. This means seeking and accepting help from a variety of sources, learning from the experience without dwelling on it, and allowing healing to gradually take place.

In my 22-year career as a city police officer, I encountered both traumatic incidents and cumulative trauma, the daily stress of policing compounding over time. I survived those experiences in the moment, but more importantly, I chose to cope positively with the effects that came after. That choice allowed me to evolve into something stronger.

The evolution of a person who has faced trauma and chooses to cope positively is remarkable. To evolve is to "develop gradually," and that is exactly what happens when we face trauma head-on. We choose not to let the trauma define us, but to be defined by how effectively we deal with it.

John Turoczi, Retired Law Enforcement Officer

Posttraumatic growth is not bouncing back.
It is rebuilding forward.

- Show up weekly. Consistency builds culture.
- Protect confidentiality. What is shared in the circle stays in the circle.
- Keep shares growth-centered: meaning-making, forward movement, and connection.
- Check on one another before leaving. If someone is in distress, pause and connect them to support.
- If suicidal or homicidal ideation is present, get higher care immediately and stay with the person until connected.

Weekly practice.
Continued growth.
Lifelong connection.

Digital Copy of the TORW PTG Group Meeting Guide

For a free digital copy of this meeting guide, please go to:

https://bticonsultingservice.com/torw

Or scan the QR code below

About the Author

Dr. Benjamin Iobst

US Army Combat Veteran, Retired Law Enforcement Officer

Ben grew up in Pennsylvania and joined the US Army shortly after September 11th, 2001. He served as an Infantryman during multiple combat tours in the Iraq War. After returning home, Ben became a police officer, serving in various roles, including Patrolman, Detective, Hostage Negotiator, Specialty Team Commander, Patrol Supervisor, and Crisis Intervention Team Supervisor. He retired from full time law enforcement in 2023.

Ben then completed his Ph.D. in Psychology and now works as an Organizational Psychology Consultant and an adjunct professor. He collaborates regularly with the mental health and substance abuse treatment community to support wellness and recovery. Due to his own struggles, as well as witnessing others' struggles, Ben is passionate about helping First Responders and Veterans, as well as spending quality time with his loving wife and two daughters. Ben continues to serve as a part-time police officer and volunteers as a peer support member with local critical incident stress management and peer wellness groups. He also holds advanced degrees in criminal justice and psychology, with extensive training in law enforcement and mental health.

About the Original Contributors

Justin Wright

USMC Combat Veteran

Justin K. Wright is a dedicated leader and advocate with a strong background in military service and community support. A former US Marine Corps Fire Team Leader who served in the Iraq War (2006-2010), he developed leadership skills through managing Marines and making complex decisions under pressure.

After his military service, Justin continued his commitment to helping others by working in the recovery field. As a Program Director, he connected the recovery community with vital resources, supervised staff, and led community outreach initiatives. Currently, as a Certified Recovery Specialist, he supports individuals recovering from substance use and collaborates with local law enforcement. Known for his strong communication, public speaking, and mentoring abilities, Justin is passionate about ethical leadership, follow-through, and fostering community wellness.

About the Original Contributors

Jeremy Gann

US Army Combat Veteran

Jeremy grew up in NW Georgia and joined the Army soon after graduating high school. He served on two deployments with the 82nd Airborne Division as a mortar gunner and team leader and later with the 1st Armored Division as a sniper and squad leader. He finished his military career in the Georgia and Oregon National Guard where he served in many roles, including as an Infantry instructor, Officer Candidate School instructor, and finally recruiting and retention. Jeremy holds a Bachelor of Arts in Organizational Leadership and a Master of Business Administration with a concentration in project management. Today he travels, hikes, plays guitar and spends time with his three children Trinity, Annabelle, and Bodhi.

About the Original Contributors

Matthew Rush

Retired Law Enforcement Officer

Matthew R. Rush is wholeheartedly dedicated to the care and well-being of First Responders. He served as a law enforcement officer with the City of Easton Police Department in numerous roles, including patrol, Field Training Officer, community outreach, training, crisis negotiator, and as a member of the Criminal Investigation Section. He also served as a sworn member of both FBI and U.S. Marshals task forces.

Matt was forced to retire as a Crimes Detective in 2021 after suffering a line-of-duty injury that led to multiple spinal and related surgeries, which have continued well beyond his retirement.

Even while still an active officer, Matt began focusing on supporting those in similar professions by advocating for officers' mental health and joining his regional Critical Incident Stress Management (CISM) Team. He was also an initial participant in forming a first-of-its-kind 1st Responder Wellness Team in the region.

Since retiring, Matt has become certified in multiple mental health and wellness training programs and regularly teaches those classes. He continues to assist First Responders following critical incidents-whether they need someone to talk to or help connecting with additional resources.

Matt is known for his hearty laugh, his ability to connect with a wide range of people, and his deep passion for First Responder wellness.

About the Original Contributors

Christopher Schierloh

Paramedic

Christopher Schierloh is a Nationally Registered Paramedic, EMS Instructor, Hazardous Materials Technician, Rope Rescue Technician, Technical Rescuer, LVLEO Coordinator, and a passionate advocate for mental health in EMS. With 15 years of experience in the civilian sector, Chris has worked with various EMS systems, including private not-for-profits, health networks, and fire/municipal-based services. Previously, Chris served as the Basic and Advanced Life Support Supervisor at West End Community Ambulance, overseeing operations,

developing training programs and guiding the agency's transition to a hospital-based system.

After the passing of his father in 2018, Chris stepped back from leadership to focus on his family, joining the busiest city EMS system within driving distance. Currently, he works as a full-time paramedic in Allentown, continually advancing as a clinical care provider, educator, and technical rescuer.

Chris is a member of the Allentown Fire Department Hazmat Team, Lehigh County Special Operations, Allentown Fire Department Technical Rescue Team, and LVLEO, and serves on the Allentown Paramedics Quality Assurance Committee. Above all, Chris is a devoted father and a playful, lighthearted presence in his children's lives.

About the Original Contributors

Adam Perreault

US Navy Veteran, Firefighter

Adam has over a decade of experience as a firefighter for the City of Allentown and Adam serves as the Commander of the Allentown Fire Department Underwater Recovery Team. As a dedicated advocate for firefighter health and safety, Adam has spent 12 years representing the IAFF Local 302 Allentown Fire Fighters Union and leads the Local 302 Peer Support Team.

After experiencing the tragic loss of a fellow firefighter to suicide, Adam played a pivotal role in establishing the Peer Support Team to educate and provide mental health resources to members. In his role as the IAFF Local 302 Legislative Director, Adam works to advance firefighter health and safety legislation at both the state and federal levels while also supporting local community groups to help build a safer, thriving Allentown. A U.S. Navy Veteran (1995–1999), Adam is a devoted Christian, husband, and father to two daughters.

Thank you for reading!

TRIBE OF THE RESTORED WARRIORS

RESOURCES FOR VETS AND FIRST RESPONDERS, BY VETS AND FIRST RESPONDERS

YOUTUBE SPOTIFY

Vets and Badges

A partner of ours in our mission for wellness is Vets and Badges, where real-life heroes share their triumphs and tribulations. For more information, please go to:

HTTPS://VETSANDBADGES.COM

www.ingramcontent.com/pod-product-compliance
Lightning Source LLC
Chambersburg PA
CBHW070918130626
46555CB00001B/189

* 9 7 9 8 9 9 4 8 0 5 1 0 7 *